SUING THE

A Practical Guid
and Enforcing

ABOUT THE AUTHORS

Chaman Salhan

Chaman is the Head of the Human Rights Department at Salhan Nijjar Solicitors (153A Corporation Street, Birmingham, B4 6PH). He studied banking and international finance at the City University Business School before completing a Diploma in Law at the City University and the legal practice course at the University of Central England. Chaman currently specialises in civil actions against the police, prisoners' rights and white collar crime.

Henry Spooner

Henry is a practising barrister of many years experience who has conducted an enormous number of criminal jury trials which have covered everything from murder to motoring matters. He has always had a particular interest in any matter which raises civil liberty issues and once practised in Australia on behalf of Aboriginal Australians. He now specialises in actions against the police and in that capacity has conducted many civil jury trials.

SUING THE POLICE

A Practical Guide to Knowing and Enforcing your Rights

Chaman Salhan
&
Henry Spooner

This book was typeset by Claire Rourke for

BLACKHALL PUBLISHING
26 Eustace Street
Dublin 2
Ireland

e-mail: blackhall@tinet.ie

ISBN: 1 901657 86 8

A catalogue record for this book is available from the British Library.

Printed in Ireland by
Betaprint Ltd

CONTENTS

DEDICATION

To all my family, but in particular to my wife Navdeep for her endless patience and my brother Madan for his years of endless support. Thank you.

Chaman

~~~
~~~

ACKNOWLEDGEMENTS

To all my past and present clients without whom this book would not have been possible.

Chaman


~~~
~~~

INTRODUCTION

Increased Police Powers

Since 1984 there has been a huge increase in police power in the UK. Indeed it is no exaggeration to say that the combined effect of the Police and Criminal Evidence Act 1984, the Public Order Act 1986 and the Criminal Justice and Public Order Act 1994, together with many other Acts, supplemented by the traditional common law powers, constitutes the greatest transfer of power from the citizen to the state since the Tudor period. Even during the national emergencies of the two world wars, it is doubtful whether the police had some of the powers they presently enjoy. These powers have been granted to the police by a willing public anxious about the 'crime wave'. Moreover, the granting of them has politically bipartisan support despite the fact that, in many important categories, crime rates have been falling for some years.

More powers are promised in forthcoming legislation. Thus the police now enjoy unprecedented power over the life of the ordinary citizen in such matters as attending football matches or other sporting activities, demonstrating on an issue of local or national importance, or attending pop festivals or raves. A gathering of more than twenty people can now, in some circumstances, be classified as an 'unlawful assembly' and animal rights protesters together with 'New Age Travellers' have been specifically targeted in legislation. There is, of course, no guarantee that these powers will not, in time, be adapted for use in other contexts. Once power is granted to the state, it is rearely, if ever, returned to the citizen.

These powers by no means stop at the front door of

a private home. 'An Englishman's home is his castle' has now gone the way of the once hallowed right of silence as a pale shadow of its former self. The police requirement to obtain a warrant prior to either search or arrest is now so diminished, and their powers to act without one so increased, that soon that protection will travel down the same road of legal tokenism. Most arrests now take place without a warrant at all. This has, in turn, been matched with court and police station procedures that have significantly shifted the balance away from the accused towards the prosecution. Securing a conviction has never been easier, and it is axiomatic that the easier it is to convict a person, the greater the chance of a miscarriage of justice.

But what options are available to a person who feels aggrieved by the actions of the police? What can a person who has been unlawfully assaulted by the police, arrested and/or imprisoned for unjustifiable reasons, or prosecuted on evidence concocted by the police, do?

Inadequate Police Accountability

In the authors' view, the increased powers of the police have not been matched by their enhanced accountability to the public. Whilst it is true that the Police Complaints Authority has been established, it is widely felt that gaining redress using this state-financed bureaucracy suffers from some serious handicaps. For example:

- Even with the injection of an 'independent element' performing a general supervisory role, the Authority has no genuinely independent investigators of its own and has to depend on other policemen to perform this function. Often if a conflict arises between the complainant and the police, the Authority will simply state that they are unable to resolve it and, therefore, the complaint fails. The perception persists that it is essentially the police investigating themselves.

- The investigation is conducted behind closed doors and often consists of a paper exercise with no actual 'hearing' at all. There is no right of representation for the aggrieved who has little or no input into the proceedings.
- Even if a complaint is upheld, there is no power to award compensation to the aggrieved party.

It is increasingly recognised that a far more satisfactory way of enforcing redress against the police, where justified, is not to rely on modern statutory machinery but instead to return to the old common law remedies established in the days prior to the formation of organised police forces, which were, traditionally, the sole source of protection of the subject against oppressive behaviour by organs of the realm. Perhaps somewhat ironically, these remedies, far from becoming increasingly redundant, are now more relevant than ever. They enjoy the following advantages.

- They guarantee a full hearing open to the public with proper representation for both parties.
- Both parties have rights of disclosure of all relevant documents in the case save for a few exceptions which the party refusing to disclose has to justify before the court.
- False imprisonment and malicious prosecution remain one of the few civil actions that can still be tried by a jury as of right.
- Successful aggrieved parties can be awarded damages to compensate them for the unlawful way they have been treated by the police. In some cases, they can be awarded extra "exemplary" damages if the court particularly disapproves of the "oppressive,

arbitrary or unconstitutional" manner in which the aggrieved party has been treated by the police.

Inadequate Legal Representation

Despite the importance of this area of the law, there is often a practical problem with the way it is handled by the legal profession. Potential cases of false imprisonment, etc. invariably arise from a failed prosecution in the criminal courts which has been handled by a busy High Street practitioner with little experience of civil cases. Yet specialist civil firms of solicitors are often reluctant to take on this type of work and in any event may have little experience of the police procedures and practices that often lie at the heart of any case against a Chief Constable. Thus, there are many people with potentially good cases against the police who fall between these two professional stools.

The coming into force of the 'Woolf Reforms' has exacerbated this problem still further. These reforms fundamentally alter many of the important pre-trial procedures with the admirable, and hopefully successful, object of speeding up the appalling length of time it takes some civil cases to come to a final hearing. The object of this book is to try and rectify these difficulties by providing:

- a concise statement of the law of the main actions against the police which are most likely to be encountered together with some of the more important police powers. This is in no sense an academic work and those requiring a deeper analysis of the law should refer to the 'standard' works on the law of tort as well as the excellent *Civil Actions Against the Police* by Clayton and Tomlinson;
- a guide as to the type and amount of damages that a successful litigant might be expected to receive;

- some helpful advice on how to commence and continue an action under the 'Woolf Reforms', together with some practical checklists;
- a guide to the sort of documents to look out for once an action is underway.

Conclusion

The overall aim of the book is to give practitioners, who may not be familiar with civil cases, the confidence to both embark on and continue with civil actions against the police where that action is justified in law.

Chaman Salhan
Salhan-Nijjar
153A Corporation Street
Birmingham
Mobile: 07050047800

Henry Spooner
Westgate Chambers
144 High Street
Lewes
East Sussex

CHAPTER 1
MAIN ACTIONS AGAINST THE POLICE

The following are the three main actions that will cover most cases against the police. They are sometimes brought separately but often involve a combination of all three. The main actions are:

- assault and battery;
- false imprisonment;
- malicious prosecution.

ASSAULT

Definition

'Assault' is simply the use of any unlawful force on one person by another. Traditionally 'an assault' is the unlawful putting of one person in fear while 'battery' is the actual use of force. However, while nearly all actions against the police involve both 'assault' and 'battery', we are using the word 'assault' to cover both concepts. Any touching which cannot in law be justified constitutes an assault.

> The fundamental principle, plain and incontestable, is that every person's body is inviolate.
>
> [per Goff L.J. in *Collins v. Wilcock* [1984] 1 W.L.R. 1173.]

Although any deliberate bodily contact that cannot in law be justified constitutes an assault, in reality a case of assault by itself would usually only be worthwhile if such unlawful contact resulted in discernible and verifiable physical injury.

Defence

The above definition of course begs the question as to what is 'unlawful'. The main defence the police will deploy is to argue that the arrest was lawful (see 'Lawfulness of the Arrest' below) and the force used was reasonable in the circumstances. They are permitted to use such force as is proportionate to the actual or anticipated resistance of the arrested person. This is judged on a common sense appraisal of not only what the police encountered, but what they might reasonably be expected to encounter. Police tactics will reasonably differ while attempting to arrest an old-aged pensioner of good character as opposed to a person with a known violent disposition. However, even in the latter case, the police must always be able to justify their actions on reasonable grounds. The court will take into account all matters in deciding whether the force used by the police was reasonable in any given circumstance.

Any force used to effect an unlawful arrest is an assault unless it is trivial [*Donnelly v. Jackman* [1970] 1 W.L.R. 562 (tapping on the shoulder)]. Even if the arrest is lawful, it is an assault if the police use unreasonable force to effect it. An arrested person is also entitled to use reasonable force to resist an unlawful arrest, and thus the legality of the arrest can often be an issue in assault cases involving the police.

The Shifting Burden of Proof

As with all civil matters, the overall burden of proof rests on the claimant to prove his/her case on the balance of probabilities. However, anyone who takes away another person's liberty must be able to justify it. Thus, the burden falls on the police to justify, in law, on a balance of probabilities, why such deprivation of a person's liberty was lawful. Therefore, in assault cases where the legality of an arrest becomes an issue, the burden of proving the unreasonableness of the force used rests on the claimant, but justifying the lawfulness of the arrest in the first place is for the police to prove on a balance of probabilities. The lawfulness of the arrest is a question of law to be decided by the judge. Whether the force used was unreasonable is a question of fact to be determined by the jury, if there is one.

FALSE IMPRISONMENT

Definition

In police cases, it is sufficient to define false imprisonment as the confinement of a person in a place against his will. It is, of course, not only the police who can falsely imprison a person; it is a criminal offence for anyone to do so. There is a body of law as to what constitutes 'imprisonment'. However, this rarely presents a problem in police cases where there is invariably no issue that the claimant was being detained against his/her will. This definition would include all circumstances where a person is obliged 'to go with' the police and not just being placed in a locked cell. Thus, being the subject of an unlawful stop and search (see Appendix 2), being driven in a police vehicle, and being placed in an unlocked room in the police station constitutes 'imprisonment' if a person has, in practice, no choice in the matter and the police are not, in law, justified in taking away that person's liberty of movement.

False imprisonment will also lie if a person is lawfully arrested but has their detention either unnecessarily prolonged or the police are in breach of the custody time limits set under the Police and Criminal Evidence Act 1984 (hereafter 'PACE', see Appendix 3 for further information).

Defence to False Imprisonment

The police will have an answer to false imprisonment if they can establish that the purported detention and arrest of a suspect is within the powers granted to them by either statute or common law. The police have been granted ever-increasing powers in recent years by various acts of parliament (in a book of this size it is quite impossible to state the enormous range of powers the police have now been given). We will deal here, firstly, with the two main general powers to arrest without warrant, and, secondly, with what the police need to show to justify an arrest.

THE POWER TO ARREST WITHOUT A WARRANT FOR AN ARRESTABLE OFFENCE

Section 24(6) states that:

> Where a constable has reasonable grounds for suspecting that an arrestable offence has been committed, he may arrest without warrant anyone whom he has reasonable grounds for suspecting to be guilty of the offence.

Section 24(7) states that:

> A constable may arrest without warrant:
>
> a) anyone who is about to commit an arrestable offence;

b) anyone whom he has reasonable grounds for suspecting is about to commit an arrestable offence.

Thus the police have power to arrest a person if they have reasonable grounds for suspecting that an arrestable offence has been, or is about to be, committed.

Arrestable Offence

This has now been extended beyond its original definition in the Criminal Law Act 1967 by section 24(2) of PACE. 'Arrestable offences' now include the following.

- Offences for which the offence is fixed by law.
- Offences where a previously convicted person over 21 years of age could be sentenced to at least five years imprisonment.
- Offences for which an arrest could be made under section 1(i) of the Customs and Management Act 1979.
- Offences under the Official Secrets Act where the maximum sentences are under five years.
- Section 14 of the Sexual Offences Act 1956 (indecent assault on a woman).
- Section 22 of the Sexual Offences Act 1956 (causing prostitution of a woman).
- Section 23 of the Sexual Offences Act 1956 (procuring of a girl under 21).
- Section 12(i) of the Theft Act 1968 (taking a motor vehicle without authority).
- Section 25(i) of the Theft Act 1968 (going equipped for theft).
- Section 1 of the Public Bodies and Corrupt Practices Act (causing the corruption of an official).

- Section 24(3) of PACE (any conspiracy, attempt, incitement, aiding, abetting, counselling or procuring the commission of an arrestable offence).

Serious Arrestable Offence

A new category of 'serious arrestable offence' has been created by PACE. The distinction between an 'arrestable' and a 'serious arrestable' offence becomes particularly important with regard to the length of time the police can lawfully hold someone in a police station without charge (see Appendix 3). Section 16 and Schedule 5 constitute the original list; this has been subsequently expanded. Below are the main 'serious arrestable' offences.

- Treason.
- Murder.
- Manslaughter.
- Kidnapping.
- Rape.
- Incest with a girl under 16.
- Buggery with a boy or non-consensual buggery with an adult (now classified as rape).
- Gross indecency.
- Intercourse with a girl under 13.
- Some offences under the Firearms Act 1968.
- Causing death by reckless driving.
- Causing an explosion likely to endanger life or property.
- Hostage taking.

- Hijacking.
- Torture.
- Offences against the Drug Trafficking Act 1971.
- Section 14(i) of the Protection of Children Act 1978.
- Section 15(2) of the Obscene Publications Act 1959.
- There are other statutory provisions relating to protection of the environment and wild animals, aviation security and the prevention of terrorism.

Furthermore, 'arrestable offences' can be converted into 'serious arrestable offences' if there is:

- serious harm to the state or public order;
- serious interference with the administration of justice;
- serious injury;
- substantial financial gain or loss to any person.

Additional Police Powers

Below are some of the additional police powers attached to a 'serious arrestable offence'.

- The grant of a search warrant under section 8 of PACE.
- The authorisation of detention without charge beyond 24 hours and with the grant of a warrant by a magistrate beyond 36 hours (see Appendix 3).
- The authorisation of a road block by a senior officer.
- Delay in the exercise of the right to inform a relative or friend of the arrest or access to legal advice

to a person detained for a 'serious arrestable offence'.

THE POWER TO ARREST WITHOUT A WARRANT FOR MINOR OFFENCES

Section 25 of PACE

This states:

> Where a constable has reasonable grounds for suspecting that any offence which is not an arrestable offence has been committed or is being committed or attempted he may arrest the relevant person if it appears to him that the service of a summons is impracticable or inappropriate because any of the general arrest conditions is satisfied.

General Arrest Conditions

These are defined in section 25(3) as follows.

- The name of the relevant person is unknown and cannot readily be ascertained by the constable.
- The constable has reasonable grounds for doubting whether a name furnished by the relevant person is the real name.
- The relevant person has failed to furnish a satisfactory address for service or the constable has reasonable grounds for doubting whether the address furnished is a satisfactory one for service.
- The constable has reasonable grounds for believing that an arrest is necessary to prevent the relevant person from causing physical harm to himself or another person, suffering physical injury, causing loss or damage to property, committing an

offence against public decency or unlawfully obstructing a highway.

- A constable has reasonable grounds for believing that an arrest is necessary to protect a child or other vulnerable person from the relevant person.

Relevant Person

This is defined in section 25(2) as:

> Any person whom the constable has reasonable grounds to suspect of having committed or having attempted to commit the offence or of being in the course of committing or attempting it.

This section is primarily intended to be used in situations where minor offences have been allegedly committed or attempted which should normally be dealt with by summons, but there are reasonable grounds for supposing that the service of such a summons is impracticable either because of doubts about the authenticity of the information supplied or the urgency of the situation. It would be for the police to justify why such service of a summons was impracticable in these circumstances and why they instead opted for an arrest without warrant.

THE POWER TO ARREST WITHOUT A WARRANT UNDER THE COMMON LAW

Thus sections 24 and 25 of PACE created new statutory powers of arrest. Section 26 of PACE repealed most of the other outstanding powers, but it retained specifically the common law powers for constables to arrest without warrant to either prevent a breach of the peace or halt a continuing one. These powers were expressly preserved by the Public Order Act 1986, section 40(4).

The common law has always given the police a wide discretion to arrest where a breach of the peace is either reasonably anticipated to occur or to prevent one from breaking out. 'Breach of the peace' is an ancient concept that embraces the constables' fundamental duty to maintain the 'Queen's peace' and can be applied to a variety of situations. Once a breach of the peace is either reasonably anticipated or has broken out, the constable may:

- take any reasonable measures necessary to prevent such a breach;
- arrest any person threatening the peace;
- temporarily restrain any person without arresting him;
- arrest a person seized by a bystander provided he has reasonable belief that the seizure was done reasonably;
- arrest any person, on the say-so of a third party, who has already committed a breach of the peace and is reasonably likely to do so again in the near future.

Thus, the police have been given a wide flexible power to meet most situations where a threat to public order is perceived or has broken out. Yet parliament has given the police even more powers to arrest without a warrant in both the Public Order Act 1986 and the Criminal Justice Act 1994, while retaining all the original common law powers. The combined effect of the common law powers still retained - PACE, the Public Order Act 1986 and the Criminal Justice and Public Order Act 1994 — means that the police have now been given the most extensive range of power since their creation in the 19th century.

Public Order Act 1986 and Criminal Justice and Public Order Act 1994

As stated, it is not possible in a book of this scope to detail the numerous new powers that the police have been given to arrest without warrant. They cover all aspects of human behaviour, not only in public, but also, increasingly, on private property as well. Any public gathering for virtually any purpose, however trivial, is now subject to police control and permission, backed up by powers of arrest without warrant for failing to comply. The 1994 Act gives senior police officers draconian powers in respect of 'New Age Travellers' (section 61), 'raves' (section 63) and 'hunt saboteurs' (section 68). A new offence of 'trespasser assembly' has been created (section 70) that severely restricts the right of free spontaneous 'assembly' (defined as over twenty people) and can now even include arrest without suspicion of an offence in some circumstances (section 60(5). There is, of course, no guarantee that powers supposedly brought in to deal with one situation would not, over time, be extended to other activities.

ARREST WITH A WARRANT

We have concentrated mainly on police powers without a warrant because these now make up the majority of police arrests and, therefore, cases against them. The one area of police activity where warrants still retain some measure of importance relates to the searching of private property without consent. This pays lip-service to 'an Englishmen's home is his castle', which today is far from an impregnable fortress. The police have been given ever-increasing powers of searching property with a warrant to help balance those they have been given without one. However, if the police cannot justify a search within the terms of their statutory powers, they would be open to an action for trespass, although in the absence of any specific damage, the damages are unlikely to be more than nominal. Whether or not the police acted lawfully in searching a property may be an important issue in other actions. In an assault case, for example, an important issue could be whether the police were entitled to be on the premises, and thus whether the occupier was entitled to eject them with reasonable force.

See Appendix 1 for a summary of the main police search powers and procedures and the appropriate *Code of Practice* under PACE.

THE LAWFULNESS OF THE ARREST

In order to justify the arrest, the officer has to satisfy two tests sometimes known as the 'Woolf Criteria' following the judgement of Woolf L.J. in *Castorina v. Chief Constable of Surrey* [(1988) New L.J. 180 (CA)].

Lord Woolf stated that three questions needed to be asked:

- **Did the arresting officer suspect that the person arrested was guilty of the offence?** A finding of fact as to the officers state of mind.
- **Was there reasonable cause for the suspicion?** An objective test. This test has been defined as:

> Whether a reasonable man, assumed to know the law and possessed with the information which in fact was possessed by the defendant (i.e. the police officer), would believe there were reasonable grounds.
>
> [per Diplock L.J. *Dallinson v. Caffrey* [1965] 1 Q.B. 348 at 371]

- If the answer to both questions is yes, has the officer fulfilled the 'Wednesbury' criteria in exercising his discretion to arrest, i.e. **has the officer reached a decision on irrational grounds, or taken matters into account that he shouldn't, or ignored matters which he should have taken into account?** This hardly ever emerges as an issue in the vast majority of police cases and we do not propose to add anything further on the last question.

The first two elements have to be present in order to constitute a lawful arrest. The first test (i.e. did the officer have a personal suspicion) rarely presents any difficulty. It would be unusual for the constable not to have such a personal belief if the second criterion is fulfilled. It is the second test (i.e. was there reasonable grounds for suspicion) that invariably forms the bedrock of cases of false imprisonment. In reaching a decision as to whether it was reasonable for the officer to have the requisite reasonable belief, only information available to the constable prior to the arrest is relevant. Thus, any subsequent information that casts the suspect in a guiltier light cannot be used to justify an unlawful arrest (although it might significantly effect quantum), just as later information which exculpates the suspect cannot render unlawful an initial lawful arrest. The court is, therefore, required to analyse carefully exactly what would or should have been the officer's state of knowledge prior to making the arrest.

Sir Frederick Lawton stated in *Castorina*:

> Suspicion by itself, however, will not justify an arrest. There must be a factual basis for it of a kind which a court would adjudge to be reasonable. When there is an issue in a trial as to whether a constable had reasonable cause, his claim to have had knowledge or to have received reports on which he relied may be challenged.

Reasonable Grounds for Suspecting

In practice, the courts have not set the police a very high hurdle over which to jump. The basic policy of the courts is to put the detection of the crime above an individual's liberty and they are reluctant to unduly hamper the police in their enquiries. [See *Hussein v. Chong Fook Cham* [1970] A.C. 942; *Ward v. Chief Constable of Avon and Somerset* (*The Times*, June 1986) and *Castorina*.] Thus, if the police are able to point the finger of suspicion at the suspect by relying on some reliable information, it is likely that it will be upheld by the courts as sufficiently justified, unless it is unduly tenuous and speculative. The police do not have to be right, but they are required to be genuine and reasonable in their held suspicion. The police are entitled to rely on the following:

- Matters which would be inadmissible in court, e.g. hearsay, including evidence from the constables. Thus, they can arrest a suspect on the say-so of another officer even though he/she may know little or nothing about the matter provided the first officer has reasonable suspicion.
- Information from members of the public provided it is "sensible and trustworthy". A paid informant, however, should be treated with "very considerable reserve".
- A suspect's criminal record, if clearly relevant to the alleged offence, although that will not of itself constitute "reasonable grounds" unless it satisfies the 'striking similarity' test as in similar fact evidence.

Thus, there is a reduced chance of success in false imprisonment cases where there is little dispute about the background information that the police had in their possession prior to making the arrest, and where the claimant is relying solely on its paucity or unreliability to constitute insufficient reasonable grounds. The issue as to whether there were reasonable grounds is a matter of law for the judge to determine. This will only require the assistance of the jury (in a jury case) where there are any factual issues to determine which go to the question of reasonable grounds, e.g. where the police are relying on their justification for the arrest on the suspicious way a person was behaving, but the person says he was not behaving suspiciously at all. It is only when that factual dispute is determined by the jury, that the judge can then rule as a matter of law whether the arrest was lawful or not. Consequently, the real issue in false imprisonment usually turns on whether the police were either wholly mistaken about the facts of the case on which they were relying to make the arrest, or were being dishonest in knowingly giving false information in order to bolster an unlawful arrest. Therefore, false imprisonment cases which actually reach court will often come down to the claimant claiming the arresting police behaved with bad faith or came to a view which a jury, knowing what the police know then, decide was not reasonable in the circumstances, and thus failed the second 'Woolf Criteria'.

The burden is placed on the officers to prove, on a balance of probability, that the plaintiff's liberty was justifiably curtailed for the same reason given for assault above, where the legality of the arrest becomes an issue.

WARRANT: PACE

'Arrest'

What constitutes an arrest in law? There is no magic formula as to what words a constable should use, but it must be made clear to the person in ordinary language that he/she is no longer free to go where they wish but must now comply with the orders of the arresting officer. This can take a variety of forms depending on the circumstances, place and the reasonably assumed or actual behaviour of the person the officer is in the process of arresting. Thus, in some circumstances, it would be appropriate for the officer to tell the arrested person to walk with him/her to the police station and, in others, for the person to be forcibly held or handcuffed. There is no requirement for the officer to formally place his/her hands on the arrested person's shoulder as is sometimes thought.

Section 28 of PACE lays down certain requirements:

- an arrest is not lawful unless the person arrested is informed that he/she is under arrest as soon as practicable after his/her arrest regardless of whether the fact of his arrest is obvious;
- no arrest is lawful unless the person arrested is informed of the ground for the arrest at the time of, or as soon as practicable after, the arrest. This can be of some importance in false imprisonment cases if the reason for the arrest has changed by the time the arrested person has reached the police station.

Surprisingly, section 28 stays silent about the requirement to caution an arrested person and thus it could be argued that, if an officer gave the correct reasons for arresting a person but completely failed to render the caution, it might still constitute a lawful arrest.

Whilst a person is entitled to use reasonable force to resist an unlawful arrest, it is rarely wise to do so in practice. It is often better to challenge the arresting officer's actions immediately, firmly and politely on arrival at the police station to the custody officer, and to ensure that the objections are noted on the custody record, although we also recognise that in practice this can be equally difficult.

An unlawful arrest constitutes both a technical assault as well as a false imprisonment although, if the correct reasons for the arrest are given on arrival at the police station and the detention is otherwise justified, then damages for this alone are likely to be nominal.

Malicious Prosecution

'Malicious prosecution' is made up of the following elements:

- there has been a prosecution;
- the prosecution was instituted by the defendant;
- the prosecution terminated in the claimant's favour;
- the defendant acted without reasonable and probable cause;
- the defendant acted maliciously.

Instituting a Prosecution

'Instituting a prosecution' is defined as "setting a judicial officer in motion". The origin of the action is usually from the moment of charge but the test of 'institution' is whoever was responsible for bringing about the false charge in the first place. Often this will be the arresting officer and other officers at the scene on whom the custody officer initially relies to justify the detention. Other officers also often rely on their colleagues' version of events to justify further detention, interview and charge of the claimant. Thus, the person responsible for starting the whole false process of prosecution is said to be the person 'instituting' it. Sometimes the 'institution' will occur at a later stage, for example where a minor charge is deliberately and wrongfully 'upgraded' at the police station to a more serious one in order to try and undermine a complaint that the suspect has made against his/her arresting officers.

'Terminated in the Claimant's Favour'

This is given a wide interpretation. Any ending of any criminal proceedings in the claimant's favour including discharge at committal, not proceeded with by Notice of Discontinuance, no evidence offered, claimant agreed to be bound over after 'not guilty' plea. Importantly, this will include a conviction on a minor charge if acquitted on a more serious one. Sometimes claimants are offered what are, in effect, 'deals' where they plead guilty to a lesser charge if a more serious one is dropped, and which they sometimes accept even though they are not guilty of anything. They do this either 'to get it over and done with' or to avoid a possible custodial sentence. Provided the other elements are satisfied, this situation will not be fatal to pursuing a case of malicious prosecution although any admission of guilt will inevitably put the question of 'favourable termination' in doubt as well as affect the credibility of the claimant. 'Favourable termination' probably does not include a matter being left on the file 'on the usual terms' or a *nolli prosequi*.

It is always preferable to get a 'not guilty' or 'case dismissed' outcome for the sake of clarity. If it is known that later proceedings against the police are contemplated, we advise that great care be taken in considering what the claimant should accept at the Magistrates Court. An incorrect decision there might handicap a good malicious prosecution from the outset.

Without Reasonable and Probable Cause

This was stated by Hawkins J. in *Hicks v. Faulkner* [1881] 8 Q.B.D. 167 to be:

> An honest belief in the guilt of the accused based on the full conviction founded upon reasonable grounds which would reasonably lead any ordinarily prudent and cautious man in the position of the accuser to the conclusion that the person charged was probably guilty of the crime imputed.

The burden of proving this negative rests on the claimant. This may seem difficult (and sometimes is in practice). However, often, as in false imprisonment, the question of whether there was an absence of reasonable and probable cause by the police in starting the prosecution against the claimant will turn on whether the arresting officer and those accompanying him/her are believed. It is, for example, highly unlikely that an officer giving dishonest evidence will be thought to possess 'reasonable and probable' cause. If combined with false imprisonment, a finding of an unlawful arrest will, of course, be helpful but not conclusive to establish this element because of the different burden of proof.

Malice

This is given its old, more general meaning. The essence of this action is the abuse of legal process against the claimant. This, inevitably, implies that something more than incompetence or even recklessness is required to be proved. It is the deliberate use of the legal process for something other than its intended purpose.

There need be no element of personal ill-will or a vendetta (although if there is one this will provide cogent evidence of 'malice'). Often, the 'malice' might stem from a desire by the officer to 'cover up' what he/she knows to be an unlawful arrest, or to bolster a weak evidential case against someone whom he/she thinks has committed an offence (e.g. by altering observation logs on a suspect who hasn't actually done what was 'hoped'). Any false evidence tendered against a person is evidence of 'malice', even against a person the police strongly and even rightly believe had committed an offence. Our system of law depends on the integrity of police evidence and not on the accuracy of their opinions.

A lack of reasonable and probable cause is evidence from which the jury can infer malice and in practice the two questions are often linked. As in false imprisonment, the trial questions often come down to the veracity of the arresting officers, but with the burden of proof resting on the claimant. By its very nature, the claimant must be alleging *mala fides* by the officers, and thus those factual issues, which the jury will determine, will often prove to be the crux of the whole case. A prosecution instituted on false evidence is almost certainly one where there is both an absence of reasonable and probable cause and the presence of malice. Similarly, if the jury were to conclude that officers behaved honestly, then malicious prosecution cannot succeed even if they were found to have been either completely mistaken or incompetent. Whilst it is possible to have a prosecution instituted without reasonable and probable cause but without malice, one often follows the other once the credibility of the police evidence has been undermined.

It is for the judge to determine whether there is any prima facie evidence of malice and for the jury to decide whether it actually existed based on the facts.

MISFEASANCE IN A PUBLIC OFFICE

We have considered above the three main actions against the police but, in recent times, there has been something of a revival in this ancient tort. It was once used mainly by electors who claimed they had been maliciously denied the right to vote by the returning officer. The common law has used the inherent flexibility of this tort to help 'fill the gaps' created by other torts. Unlike both false imprisonment and malicious prosecution, neither an arrest nor a prosecution is required to be present in order to establish an action. In theory, it can apply to all manner of situations beyond the confines of the arrest and prosecution, and indeed without involving the police at all, provided the person sued comes within the category of a 'public officer'.

Elements

Elements are defined in *Three Rivers District Council et al. v. Governor of the Bank of England* (*The Times*, 22 April 1996) as:

- The tort of misfeasance in a public office was concerned with a deliberate and dishonest wrongful abuse of the powers given to a public officer.
- 'Malice', in the sense of an intention to injure the claimant, combined with a knowledge that he had no power to do the act complained of, or reckless as to whether he had the powers or not.
- The tort can be committed by acts of omission as well as commission.
- The purpose of the tort was to give compensation to those who had suffered loss as a result of improper abuse of power. The matter has now come before the Court of Appeal (*The Times*, 10 December 1998). The Court has held that, in every case, there had to be a deliberate and dishonest abuse of power by an official who knew that the claimant would suffer loss as a result, or who was recklessly indifferent to that result.

Can this tort be used as an alternative to other remedies against the police?

i) An Alternative to Malicious Prosecution

This issue arose in *Silicott v. Commissioner of Police for the Metropolis* (Unreported, 24 May 1996) where the claimant's main complaint was that an officer had falsified evidence against him and that false evidence had formed the basis of the charge of the murder of PC Blakelock during the Tottenham Broadwater Farm riot. The main advantage of bringing misfeasance as an alternative to malicious prosecution is that it would spare the claimant the need to prove the absence of reasonable and probable cause which, as we have seen, can sometimes prove difficult for a claimant. In that case, it was held that misfeasance was not an exception to the 'immunity rule' which states that no action lies against parties or witnesses for anything said or done, however falsely or maliciously, in a court of law. There is a similar protection for Members of Parliament at Westminster. This proposition is also supported in *Marrinan v. Vibart* [1963] 1 Q.B. 528.

The public policy reasons for this immunity are to:

- protect people in court from having to defend themselves against further actions for what they are saying in court, thus making them likely to be more forthcoming in their evidence;
- avoid the possibility of different courts coming to different conclusions over the same evidence.

The 'immunity rule' applies to criminal proceedings but does not extend to matters outside the relevant proceedings. It specifically does not apply in malicious prosecution, malicious abuse or malicious arrest, which constitute specific exceptions to it. However, in cases where the plaintiff's case relies on what was said previously in another court, it was held that misfeasance was not to be used by plaintiffs as a handy way to by-pass the necessity to prove the absence of reasonable and probable cause. In other words, the claimant must get home on malicious prosecution or not at all. The immunity rule was not to be further breached in those circumstances. This strict application of the rule greatly restricts the scope of bringing this action as an alternative to malicious prosecution.

ii) An Alternative to False Imprisonment

It is submitted that misfeasance can coexist with false imprisonment where there is no judicial process being challenged and thus no necessity to prove the absence of reasonable and probable cause for the prosecution. However, if the arrest is alleged to be unlawful, it would be simpler to allege false imprisonment alone where not only are the legal principles more clearly defined, but the burden of proof rests on the defendant to justify the legality of the arrest in the first place. There is also no requirement to prove malice.

Misfeasance can, in theory, be useful where the initial arrest was lawful but the motive was malicious. However, in practice, this would often be hard to prove. The claimant would have to establish that the officer had a hidden personal agenda in making the arrest. The fact that the arrest was justified would in any event affect both credibility and quantum. Yet misfeasance might have some practical use in cases where there are allegations of unreasonable 'targeting' and harassment of a person with a known criminal record by the police (see 'Stop and Search' in Appendix 2) in breach of the relevant code of practice.

Misfeasance as a 'Stand Alone' Action

Misfeasance is an appropriate tort to consider where the alleged police misconduct is not related to either an arrest or a prosecution. Freed from the necessity to either require a prosecution or an unlawful arrest, this tort is given a flexibility denied to others. It can be applied to a variety of situations where a person claims he/she has suffered an abuse of police power, but which falls short of an arrest. It can thus be useful in plugging the gaps that other torts cannot fill.

Examples

- Where a police officer has used his official position to obtain an unfair personal advantage, e.g. by threatening to arrest a neighbour (but not actually doing so) over a personal dispute with him or his family.
- Where a police officer uses his position to effect a personal vendetta, e.g. following a businessperson, with whom he was having a personal dispute, in full uniform to put off the businessperson's customers.
- A continued campaign to 'stop and search' a person on the basis that it was thought 'he was up to something', or because he had an ongoing complaint against the police. This would probably be better brought as a single action of misfeasance rather than multiple actions for assault and false imprisonment.
- Improper use of the police computer in breach of the Data Protection Act 1995, if damage and malice can be proved.
- Misfeasance can be considered where a person has been lawfully arrested but not prosecuted, provided damage and malice can be proved. In *Braeggar v. Commissioner of Police for the Metropolis* (Unreported, Central London County Court), it was held to be a misfeasance for the police to keep a known claustrophobic who was lawfully arrested (thus no false imprisonment) in a locked cell against the advice of the police surgeon, in an attempt to induce a con-

fession from her mother whom they had also lawfully arrested. Similarly, an unjustified strip search in breach of the guidelines following a lawful arrest (thus no false imprisonment), but which involved no touching by the police (and thus no assault), might be considered misfeasance if the other elements could be established. Likewise, the refusal to destroy fingerprints after an acquittal might be another such case, particularly if those fingerprints went on to form the basis of another unjustified arrest.

CHAPTER 2
DAMAGES

GENERAL DAMAGES: COMPENSATORY

The courts have found it hard to compensate either satisfactorily or consistently for what are in effect breaches of civil rights. In the absence of a written constitution, the courts have attempted an amalgam of personal injury and defamation principles combined with the use of old common law concepts of aggravated and exemplary damages. Where there has been pain and suffering and loss of amenity, an equation can be made with personal injury cases. However, how do you satisfactorily compensate for such things as loss of liberty, personal humiliation and long-lasting or even permanent distrust and fear of the police? To add to the difficulty, judges were only permitted to give juries the most basic general guidance in which figures were not mentioned. The consequence was that awards varied enormously from cases that appeared factually similar. This trend was noticeable not only in cases where juries were used but also where judges sat alone. This was particularly the situation with the award of exemplary damages where, in some instances, huge awards were made.

In an attempt to bring more consistency into quantum in this area of the law, the Court of Appeal laid down guidelines in *Thompson v. Commissioners of Police for the Metropolis* and *HSU v. The Same* (Times Law Reports 19 February 1997; see below under 'Thompson Guidelines').

As far as compensatory damages are concerned, the

usual personal injury guidelines apply as to remoteness and plaintiff's duty to mitigate his/her loss. However, compensatory damages, as opposed to aggravated and exemplary damages, should not be adversely affected by the claimant's conduct. Thus, in *Millington v. Metropolitan Police Commissioner* (*The Times*, 28 May 1983), an award was made to "an engaging scoundrel whose acquaintance with the truth was minimal". In *Lane v. Holloway* [1968] 1 Q.B., Salmon L.J. stated that the fact that the plaintiff behaved badly was irrelevant to the question of compensatory damages.

Each case will turn on its separate facts but we list below the sort of factors to be taken into account when considering the main actions. It is not an exclusive list and many of the matters will overlap each other if more than one type of action is brought in one case.

Assault

The following matters might be taken into account when assessing compensatory damages:

- Any physical injury sustained.
- Nervous shock (can be claimed for assault without battery).
- Post traumatic stress disorder in the case of a serious assault.
- Aggravated damages (see below).

False Imprisonment

The following matters should be taken into account:

- Time spent in custody.
- Loss of reputation.

- Anxiety about being locked up.
- Whether or not an apology was received from the police.
- Aggravated damages (see below).
- Exemplary damages (see below).

Malicious Prosecution

The following matters should be taken into account:

- Time spent in custody after charge.
- Time spent on all court appearances until moment of favourable termination.
- Anxiety when awaiting the outcome of criminal trial, particularly if custodial sentence is an almost certainty or possibility on conviction.
- Loss of reputation, particularly if the charge involved accusations of dishonesty or sexual misconduct.
- Publicity that the charge and court appearances attracted.
- The presence or absence of an apology from the police.
- Bail conditions while awaiting trial.
- Whether or not post traumatic stress disorder had been caused.
- Aggravated damages (see below).
- Exemplary damages (see below).

Aggravated Damages

This has been defined by Lord Diplock in *Broome v. Cassell & Company* [1872] A.C. 1027 as:

> Compensation for the injured feelings of the plaintiff where his sense of injury resulting from the wrongful physical act is justifiably heightened by the manner in which or motive for which the defendant did it.

It was further defined in *Thompson v. Commission of Police for the Metropolis* [Times Law Reports 19 February 1997] as:

> Aggravating features could include such humiliating features at the time of the arrest or any conduct of those responsible for the arrest or the prosecution which showed that they had behaved in a high-handed, insulting, malicious or oppressive manner either in relation to the arrest or imprisonment or in conducting the prosecution. Aggravating features could also include the way litigation and trial were conducted.

This award, if appropriate, is in addition to the 'basic award' (see below), but is still designed to compensate the claimant rather than punish the defendant. The claimant's character and conduct can effect the amount awarded under this heading.

The following matters should be taken into account:

- Arrest in a public place with many onlookers.
- Arrest outside home in front of neighbours.
- Arrest at home in front of wife/husband/partner/parents and own children and other members of the family to their distress.

- Lack of an apology from the police.
- Lack of politeness while being detained.
- Racial, gender or homophobic abuse.
- Whether or not the plaintiff was strip-searched.
- Whether or not intimate samples were taken.
- Whether or not the plaintiff's children were placed on the 'at risk' register as a consequence of the false charge.
- Whether or not there were any family proceedings as a consequence of the false charge.
- Whether or not the plaintiff was placed on a child abuse register as a consequence of the false charge(s).
- Conduct of police in informing employers, social services and other members of the family or community about the nature of the charges.
- The effect on present and future employment prospects.
- The seriousness of the charges and the likelihood of receiving a custodial sentence.
- Whether or not a custodial sentence was given on the charge prior to its quashing on appeal.
- The degree of publicity the matter received in the press.
- Whether or not there was a diagnosis of post traumatic stress disorder as a consequence of the charge(s).

Exemplary Damages

This has been defined as:

> Oppressive, arbitrary or unconstitutional action by servants of the government.

Unlike the other awards, this is designed to punish the defendant (even though its effect is a windfall for the claimant) for his/her oppressive and arbitrary actions against the claimant. Exemplary damages can be awarded if the jury or judge so disapprove of the behaviour of the police that they feel the combined basic and aggravated award is an insufficient expression of their disapproval.

THE THOMPSON GUIDELINES

As indicated above, in an attempt to try and bring some conformity into the awards in this area, the Court of Appeal issued guidelines in the case of *Thompson v. Commissioner of Police for the Metropolis* and *HSU v. The Same* (Times Law Reports 19 February 1997).

The guidelines state:

> The jury should be told initially that there are 'ordinary damages' that should be described as the 'basic damages'. In addition, there would be 'aggravated damages' and 'special damages' for specific items of pecuniary loss.

Basic Damages

False Imprisonment

In a straightforward case of wrongful arrest and imprisonment, the starting point should be £500 for the first hour. An additional sum on a reducing scale should be awarded for all subsequent hours. For someone kept in custody for 24 hours, the figure suggested is £3,000.

Malicious Prosecution

The figure should start at £2,000. For a prosecution continuing for two years and which goes to the Crown Court, an award of £10,000 could be appropriate. If the malicious prosecution was set aside on appeal then a larger sum could be awarded to reflect the longer period of time the plaintiff had been in 'peril'.

Aggravated Damages

Where aggravated damages are deemed appropriate "the figure was unlikely to be less than £1,000".

> It was not possible to indicate a precise arithmetical relationship between basic damages and aggravated damages because the circumstances would vary from case to case, but ordinarily the court would not expect the aggravated damages to be as much as twice the basic damages.

Exemplary Damages

The jury should be told that these should only be awarded if they consider that both the basic and aggravated awards were in total an inadequate punishment for the defendant's high-handed and oppressive behaviour towards the claimant. However, they should be no more than was required to show the jury's disapproval of the police conduct. Where exemplary damages were appropriate, they were unlikely to be less than £5,000. The conduct "would have to be particularly deserving of condemnation for an award as much as £25,000". For an officer involving the rank of at least superintendent, the "absolute maximum" should be £50,000.

Claimant's Conduct

In an appropriate case, the jury should be told that, even though the claimant succeeded on liability, any improper conduct by the claimant could either reduce or eliminate any aggravated or exemplary damage - but not the basic award - especially if his/her conduct in some way contributed to the police's conduct complained of.

These guidelines should be upgraded in line with inflation. It was emphasised that these were only guidelines and juries were free to depart from them because of the considerable variations from case to case. The awards should not be approached in a mechanical way. The one suggested maximum was for exemplary damages of £50,000, although it is not impossible for that sum to be exceeded as well.

CHAPTER 3
FUNDING LITIGATION: WHO TAKES THE RISK?

Litigation can be very expensive. Accordingly, the issue of how a case is to be paid for needs to be resolved at the very outset of any case. The solicitor for his part will require assurances that he/she is going to be paid for the work that he/she undertakes, whilst the client will need to work out what the ultimate cost will be.

There are principally three ways of funding a case.

1. The client pays privately.
2. The client enters into a conditional no win no fee arrangement.
3. The client qualifies for legal aid.

Each of these methods will now be considered in turn.

PAYING PRIVATELY

This is perhaps the simplest method of instructing a solicitor, as the client merely agrees to pay the solicitor's reasonable costs of fighting the case. What amounts to 'reasonable' will be discussed at the outset, and the solicitor will quote his/her hourly fee as well as estimating the time that he/she thinks the matter will take to be concluded.

The payment of the fees normally occurs by way of staged payments through interim and final bills. The client will note that he/she will be liable for the costs of his solicitor regardless of whether the case is won or lost.

This system of funding is considered to be outdated in litigation cases, as the client undertakes all of the risk. Many clients believe that their solicitors should share some of the risk, if not all of it. This shift in risk is now possible through the adoption of a 'no win no fee' conditional arrangement.

CONDITIONAL FEES

Under this method of funding, a client buys an insurance policy to protect himself/herself against any adverse cost implications that may apply. The insurance policy will not pay the solicitor's costs should he/she lose the case, but will pay the legal costs incurred by the police. Further, the insurance policy will not pay for any disbursements (i.e. costs of preparing medical reports). The cost of the disbursements will therefore have to be met by the client himself/herself or alternatively by the solicitor. Clearly, the problem with this method of funding is that the solicitor (who ultimately is a businessman) will only take on a case if he/she is certain to win. Also, insurance companies will charge higher premiums in cases where the risks of losing are higher, to protect themselves. The actual premium itself is irrecoverable whether you win or lose; under this method, the solicitor takes on some of the risk.

Where a case is taken on, the issue of 'risk' still has implications for the client, even if he/she wins. Under the conditional fee scheme, the solicitor will be entitled to charge a risk premium, which he/she will be able to recover direct from the client. In effect this premium works by way of a mark up on his costs and is an additional payment to the solicitor to compensate him/her for taking on the risk in the first place. The solicitor would, for example, be able to say to the client that should he/she win the case a premium of 100 per cent will apply. The effect of this is perhaps best seen by way of an example.

> Example 1
>
> Mr A sues the police for false imprisonment and malicious prosecution. The solicitor thinks the client has a 50/50 chance of success and suggests that a 100 per cent premium apply to his costs. The client agrees to this. Insurance is bought for the client should he/she lose the case. The matter is contested and proceeds to trial. Mr A wins and is awarded damages of £50,000. The solicitor's legal costs are £15,000 and are paid by the other side. In addition to this, the solicitor would say to his client that he/she should receive his premium, which in effect is 100 per cent of the £15,000, namely a further £15,000. This premium will not be recoverable from the other side. Ultimately, the solicitor therefore will receive £30,000 by way of costs and the client receives £35,000 (£50,000 - £15,000).

Clients should be wary of the premium being charged by their solicitor, and should be fully appraised of the implications of it before agreeing to it. The solicitor should ensure that a note is kept of the explanation and that a letter confirming it, and a signed agreement authorising it are kept on the file.

It will be noted that under the new Access to Justice Bill, which is currently before parliament, it is proposed that the risk premium should be made recoverable in the future. A client should ensure that his solicitor advises him/her of any development in the law that allows this to occur. Solicitors also should be careful that, when the new rules come into force, they do not take money from their clients, but instead look to recover it from the other side. The Bill is not likely to become law until the year 2000.

LEGAL AID

The Present System

The eligibility for legal aid is currently tested using two distinct tests; with the client needing to pass both tests before legal aid can be given. The first test is a means test, which seeks to establish whether the client has enough money to fund the case on a private, fee-paying basis. The client will, accordingly, be asked a series of questions, which will form the basis of the assessment, by the Legal Aid Board. It will be noted that, if a false statement is made by the client, he/she may be brought before the Magistrates Court in respect of an allegation of attempting to obtain legal aid by providing false information. The solicitor should advise the client of this and should as a matter of good practice ask the client to complete the form himself/herself.

The second test looks at the merits of the client's case. The Legal Aid Board will want to see whether the client has a case and what his likely prospects of success are. The test applied by the Board is "would the client spend his own money on fighting the case, if he/she had it". By implication it is suggested that a private, fee-paying client would not fight a case unless he/she thought he/she had more than a 50 per cent chance of success.

The Legal Aid Board can agree to allow a client legal aid as long as he/she contributes to it. This will only occur where the Legal Aid Board believes there to be a certain level of disposable income that can be used towards the legal costs. If the client wins his case, some of this will be recoverable. In cases such as this, the Legal Aid Board will usually make an offer of legal aid that the client will need to accept and subsequently return to the Board together with the first cheque for the amount of contribution. Should a client fall behind on his payments, legal aid can be revoked or discharged.

Accordingly in cases such as this, the solicitor should try to ensure that the work is done as quickly as possible.

If the client qualifies for legal aid, it can affect the position of costs at the end of the case. In effect if the client loses the case, the court will have to decide if it should award costs against the client. If he/she has legal aid, then the court is unlikely to agree to do this. Even if the court does, the costs normally will not be enforceable against the client without the leave of the court. Ultimately, the client is, therefore, still protected to some degree as the risk of the litigation is taken on by the state.

This can also have a bearing on the way in which the police decide to proceed with the case. If they know, for example, that they are unlikely to recover their costs, then they may be more willing to settle the case.

The Proposed New System

If the government has its way, the whole system of legal aid is going to change substantially in the future. The proposals for change are contained in the Access to Justice Bill, which is referred to above. In particular it is proposed that the Legal Aid Board is to be replaced by the Legal Services Commission, which itself will be subdivided into the Criminal Defence Service and the Community Legal Service (CLS). The CLS will have complete control over the administration and funding of civil legal aid.

The agenda for the CLS will be two-fold:

- to improve the poor level of advice currently available;
- to manage the legal aid budget more efficiently.

Both of these proposed measures will have a direct effect on clients and solicitors pursuing actions against the police. In particular, under the first of the criterion, the CLS will be given new powers to fund facilities, such as conciliation and mediation, in an attempt to circumvent the need to embark on costly litigation. This idea of sorting the problem out before it gets to court is expanded on at page 60.

The CLS will be expected to plan the overall budget, on both national and regional levels, of the legal aid budget. This will work by the Lord Chancellor setting two budgets for civil legal aid; which will be divided into the categories of family law and other civil legal aid. Once the budgets have been established, certain cases will be given priority and for them legal aid will effectively be guaranteed. Unfortunately for the readers of this book, this guaranteed area will not include actions against the police. Having accounted for those cases, the remaining legal aid budget will then be divided into the relevant regional offices.

In actions against the police, a solicitor will need to apply to the regional office to obtain part of this budget. In addition to the regional funding, a special centralised fund will also be set up to deal especially with cases of public importance. Thankfully, this fund will include actions against the police, as they are believed to be the type of cases from which the public will want to benefit. Accordingly, a solicitor will be able to apply to this centralised fund in addition to the regional fund.

Another proposed change under the CLS will be the recognition that solicitors will be expected to provide a specified quality of service and in effect be 'kite-marked' in their area of expertise. The kite-mark will be the franchise. Once the franchise has been obtained by the solicitor, the Legal Aid Board will consider whether to award a contract to him/her. If a contract is granted, the solicitor will agree to conduct a certain number of cases in this field in exchange for a set level of legal aid. Once granted, the contract will remain in force for a period of three years.

In the future, clients who want to pursue actions against the police will have to find solicitors who have a contract and who are prepared to take their case on under the legal aid scheme. Once that has been done, the client will have to be vetted to see whether he/she qualifies for legal aid in any event. In this regard the new funding regime adopts tighter criterion for the means test and specifically looks at whether:

a) mediation could be used;

b) an alternative method of funding is available;

c) a private client would take the matter on.

The issues raised by this new test have far-reaching implications for clients seeking to get legal aid. Particularly, in respect of point (b) above, the proposed test will include a section asking whether a conditional fee arrangement is suitable. Under the new guidelines, if a solicitor replies "no" to this question, the Legal Aid Board may approach another firm of solicitors and ask them whether they would be prepared to take the case on instead on a 'no win no fee' arrangement. Accordingly, a firm of solicitors which is more risk-seeking than risk-averse may prosper under the new proposals. As to point (c), the CLS may impose a strict risk return trade-off in cases which have only a marginal chance of winning. The way in which this would work is that it would be assumed that a private paying client would not take on a risky case unless the possible return by way of damages greatly exceeded the likely cost of the case. In such cases, ratios in the region of one to four may apply to costs as compared to the level of damages to be recovered.

Even if all of the above criteria are satisfied by the client, he/she still faces one last hurdle which is, in fact, the most strict. This relates to the merit of pursuing the case. This, in itself, appears to be harmless until the principle behind it is considered. In that regard, the CLS will have the power to consider the merits of the case in light of the other constraints that are made on the budget. What this in effect means is that, if the regional office of the CLS and the central fund have already spent their money, the application for legal aid will be refused regardless of how strong the case is.

From the above proposed changes, it can be seen that, if the Bill is passed (as it is expected to be), it might become difficult in some circumstances for clients to obtain legal aid. Solicitors will accordingly need to make a conscious decision about whether or not they will be prepared to look at alternative methods of funding, such as the conditional fee arrangements in these types of cases. Solicitors will need to become experts in managing and controlling risk.

CHAPTER 4
INITIAL WORK TO BE DONE BY THE SOLICITOR

The need for solicitors to become experts at evaluating the risk of a case has already been discussed in Chapter 3. One of the best ways of evaluating this is to obtain counsel's opinion on the merit of proceeding in order to get maximum benefit from it. The solicitor will need to ensure that he/she gathers as much evidence as possible so that counsel can properly advise on the case. If the solicitor has failed to get the necessary information, it may cause one of two problems: counsel may give inaccurate advice, or counsel may ask the solicitor to make more enquiries. Both of these situations are unsatisfactory.

It is thus very important that the solicitor gets as much supporting evidence as he/she can. Below is a list of the type of things the solicitor should look for at this stage.

POLICE DOCUMENTS TO LOOK FOR

Custody Record

This is a crucial document as it will provide invaluable information on the following areas.

- Time of arrest.
- Circumstances surrounding the arrest.
- Time spent in custody.
- Whether the client was charged.
- Whether the client was represented by a solicitor.

- Details of any injury to the client.
- Confirmation of whether the client was seen by the police surgeon and, if so, details of any injury.
- Records of any property seized.
- A record of whether there had been a search at any other address.
- The address of the client.
- The client's height.
- The type of clothing worn by the client when arrested.
- The occupation given by the client at the time of the arrest.
- Whether there are any warrants authorising further detention.
- The identity of the arresting officer.
- Details of reviews made.
- Whether or not the Police and Criminal Evidence Act 1984 was complied with.

As can be seen from the above list, this document carries a mass of information which is particularly important in cases where false imprisonment is alleged and in cases of assault followed by detention. Its use, however, is in no way limited to these areas. Take, for example, a case in which there has been an apparent confession. In this type of case, it is of fundamental importance to ascertain whether a solicitor was present during the interview and, if so, what time he/she arrived and the length of consultation he/she had. Additionally, it will be important to note whether the police made any visits to the client's cell before the interview, during which they had at least the potential to influence the client into confessing.

Accordingly, this document should be obtained as a matter of course. A solicitor may obtain the document by writing to the police station where the client was detained and requesting it.

Tape of Interview

In all but a few cases, everyone who is arrested will be interviewed on tape and questioned about their involvement in the offence for which they have been detained. Obviously the tape will give an indication about how the police viewed the crime and how they thought the client was involved. This can often show whether or not the police had reasonable grounds on which to arrest and detain the client. In addition, the tape should make reference to any search that has been carried out and should outline how any injury (if one has arisen) has occurred.

Finally, the tape will provide a record of what the client has said, if anything, about the circumstances surrounding his arrest, detention and treatment while in police care. At the end of every interview, the police normally hand a note to the client that explains how he/she can obtain a copy of the tape. Usually, the note contains a reference number with details of the local police librarian. The solicitor should send a letter to the librarian requesting a copy of the tape and giving details of the reference number.

Prosecution Papers

If the matter proceeds to court, it is likely that some papers would have been prepared for use in the proceedings. If the matter remained in the Magistrates Court, the papers would be the documents provided by way of advance disclosure. If the matter proceeded to the Crown Court, the solicitor will have a full committal file consisting of witness statements, exhibits and unused material. All of these papers should be considered as they set out the strength of the case against the client. They also may show inconsistencies in the police case, and may provide the basis for a potential action.

In addition to these papers, and in the more serious enquiries, the police will normally have prepared a running log of all the information they have collated. This is known as the 'Holmes computer log'. If the case is a serious one, the solicitor should try to get a copy of the Holmes log, as it often indicates other possible lines of enquiry that the police may have chosen to skate over. This is particularly important as the police will often claim immunity to a lot of this material and prevent the solicitor from getting access to it at a later stage. (See 'Public Interest Immunity' in Chapter 6.)

Photographs

This largely applies to cases where there is an allegation of assault or of damage to property. In such cases, it is always useful to be able to show the full extent of the injury or damage. Photographs should be taken by a credible source who is willing to attend court if the need arises.

Exhibits

Any exhibits, both relied on in the original trial or referred to in the police inquiry, particularly if put to the claimant in the record of interview, should be obtained.

Forensic Evidence

Any forensic reports which are used in the course of the original police enquiry, particularly if not used by the police on the basis that they are 'unhelpful' to their case.

GATHERING INFORMATION FOR THE CLAIMANT'S CASE

We list here checklists for the three main actions. We realise that whilst, in most cases they are fairly obvious, nevertheless, we hope they will prove to be a useful aide memoire.

Assault

Get an account of what actually occurred, particularly who said what to whom. These are the sort of details that often fade with time and may prove useful later.

- Was the client verbally aggressive towards the police? If so, what was said?
- Had the client been drinking? If so, how much was consumed?
- Was the client co-operative with the police?
- Was the arrest resisted? If so, why?
- What did the client physically do to the police?
- Was the client punched by the police?
- Was the client kicked by the police?
- Were the police verbally aggressive towards the client? If so, what was actually said?
- Were handcuffs used? If so, was this resisted?
- Was the client assaulted after being handcuffed?
- Was the client assaulted after agreeing 'to come quietly', even if initially resisting arrest?
- Were any injuries sustained? If so, what injuries?

- Was the client medically examined at the police station by the police surgeon?
- Did the client complain to anyone else at the police station? If so, to whom, and what, if anything, was done about it?
- What was the nature of the complaint made?
- Did the client visit his/her general practitioner afterwards? If so, get the client to sign an authority to obtain a medical report.
- Were photographs taken at the police station?
- Were photographs taken by anyone else after release from detention?
- If the assault allegation is recent and injuries are still visible, the client should be professionally photographed as soon as possible.
- Did anyone else observe the client's injuries?
- How was the client treated in the police car/van?
- How was the client treated at the police station?
- Was the client strip-searched? If so, what was the reason given for the strip search?
- Were blood and other samples taken? If so, what were the reasons given for this? Was anything said about the consequences of not consenting to the taking of such samples?

False Imprisonment

Generally, obtain as much detail as possible about the background to the arrest, to form an initial view on whether or not a reasonable person would consider an arrest justifiable.

- What were the full background circumstances that led up to the arrest?
- Was the client told that he/she was under arrest? If so, what was the stated reason for the arrest?
- Was the client cautioned? If so, what did the client say in reply, if anything?
- Did the client ever protest his/her innocence? If so, what were the actual words used? How often were the words said, and to whom?
- What did the arresting officer say to the custody officer about what the client was alleged to have done? Was this the same, or similar, to what had been said to the client on arrest?
- Was the client interviewed?
- How long was the client detained?
- Did the client ask for a solicitor? If so, how much time elapsed before a solicitor arrived? Was the solicitor from the firm requested? Was the client pressured to dispense with a solicitor, e.g. told that asking for a solicitor would delay matters unnecessarily?
- Was the period of detention reviewed?
- Was the client bailed to return on another date? If so, what was the reason given?
- What effect did the detention have on the client?

Malicious Prosecution

Generally, obtain as much detail as possible about the circumstances which led to the failed prosecution and its consequences for the client.

- Was the client convicted of any offence? If this was the main charge against the client then it is highly unlikely that there will be a case for malicious prosecution.
- Did the client agree to be bound over without a plea of guilty? This will not affect an action.
- Were the charges 'left on the file on the usual terms'? If this was the main charge, it will probably prove fatal to an action for malicious prosecution.
- Was the client convicted of a significantly lesser charge than that with which he/she was originally charged?
- What was the client charged with at the police station?
- Were the charge(s) changed at court? If so, what were the charges, and how had they changed?
- Does the client still have the charge sheet and any other documentation given to him/her by the police or court?
- Was the case discontinued prior to a hearing? If so, does the client still have the Notice of Discontinuance?
- How often was the client required to attend court prior to the actual hearing?
- Was the client remanded in custody?
- What were the conditions of bail, if any? Did these conditions hamper the client significantly either in employment terms, or socially?
- Did the client give evidence?
- Did the client call defence witnesses? If so, it is important to trace them as soon as possible.

- Were there exhibits at the trial? If so, it is important to retrieve them as soon as possible.
- Was the defence case put on behalf of the client at the criminal trial the same as the client is now putting forward to you?
- Was the acquittal on a legal technicality as ordered by the judge or was it based on facts as found by the bench or jury?
- What effect did the prosecution have on the client?
- Was there any local or national publicity arising from the charges and the trial?
- Did members of the public, as a result of the case, abuse the client?
- Did the client suffer financial loss as a consequence of the charge, remand and original criminal case?

Witness Statements

Many people only have a short memory. It is imperative, therefore, that the solicitor meets with witnesses as soon as practicable so that they can remember as much as possible about the incident. The solicitor should contact anyone who:

- witnessed the circumstances which led to the client's detention;
- witnessed the assault on the client, if one occurred;
- could cast light on the way the police behaved at this time (particularly in situations where mass arrests are involved);
- could corroborate the degree of loss sustained.

It is important that the solicitor determines early on who needs to be seen. Often, delay in these types of matters can result in a witness disappearing, and this could affect the whole case.

Expert Reports

If there is any allegation of assault or psychological after-effects, it is important to obtain a professional report on the extent of this as soon as possible. Obviously, counsel will be unable to advise on the level of damages, until the extent of the problem is known. Further, if it is decided that proceedings need to be issued, the report will need to be annexed to the particulars of claim. The new rules affect this and should be considered before instructing any expert (they are discussed later, see Chapter 6).

Instructions to Counsel

Once all of the above documentation has been received, the solicitor should instruct counsel to advise generally on the merits of the action and on the issue of quantum. It should be noted that instructions to counsel should be detailed and should set out both the police case and the client's case. Any evidence supporting the client's case should be mentioned before, finally, turning to the issue of its value. At this stage, any evidence confirming the degree of loss should be included.

A client may wish to see the instructions that are being sent out by the solicitor to ensure that everything that should be said is set out in them. The client should, however, be prepared to note that the solicitor might include things in the instructions that go against the client. These need to be included so as to allow a proper assessment of risk to occur.

On receiving counsel's advice, the solicitor should know whether or not there is a case. If there is no case, the solicitor will notify the Legal Aid Board and claim for the work done. If there is a case, the solicitor will need to send a letter, before action, to the Chief Constable of the police force concerned, setting out in detail the case as he sees it against the officers. The solicitor will then need to give the police enough time to consider the facts and determine whether there was any impropriety by officers. If the police accept that there was impropriety, the only issue will be one of settling the case with an acceptable level of compensation. If, on the other hand, the police refuse to accept liability, the solicitor will need to notify the Legal Aid Board of the police stance and annexe a copy of counsel's advice. The Legal Aid Board will then decide whether they are prepared to extend legal aid to cover the cost of taking the matter to court. If legal aid is extended, the solicitor will need to send the papers back to counsel so that he can prepare the documentation necessary to lodge the action at court.

WHO TO SUE

Chief Constables are vicariously liable for all acts committed by his/her police officers in the course of their duties as police constables. Thus they should always constitute the main defendant. Sometimes claimants are keen to join as second, or subsequent defendants, any named officers they have particular reason to remember, e.g. officers who have assaulted or humiliated them. However we advise that unless there is a particular reason for doing this that this temptation should be resisted. This is for two main reasons.

- Once officers have been so named then they become a separate party and as such are entitled to have their own input into the conduct of the proceedings. This can often have the effect of hampering a reasonable settlement proposed by the Chief Constable. Once officers are specifically named as defendants, they often feel, not unreasonably, that it is important both to them and their future careers 'to clear their name' and thus their personal agendas can sometimes be at odds with that of their Chief Constable.

- Sometimes claimants get genuinely confused as to the identity of officers particularly in fast moving situations and this can present all manner of evidential and pleading problems. Indeed it is better not to mention officers' names at all unless the claimant can be completely certain who is who in any given situation.

ENTITLEMENT TO A JURY TRIAL

One of the most important features of these case is that it is now one of the few civil matters where the right of a jury has been retained. The position for the main actions is as follows.

False Imprisonment and Malicious Prosecution

Sections 69(1) of the Supreme Court Act 1981, for the High Court, and 66(3) of the County Courts Act 1984, for the County Court, specifically give a claimant a right of jury trial in these actions. Both the Acts contain a proviso which states that, if the court is of the opinion that the trial requires any prolonged examination of documents or accounts or any scientific or local investigation which cannot be made with a jury, then the court can try the matter by judge alone. However, this is rarely if ever, likely to occur with actions against the police and any objection to a jury trial citing this ground by the defendant should in our view be strenuously resisted.

- This right to a jury trial is granted to either side so that a defendant can insist on a jury trial even if the claimant does not want one, although the authors have not come across this situation in police cases.

- Either party can waive their right to a jury trial and opt for a judge only one.

Other Actions

The above Acts give the entitlement to jury trial in false imprisonment and malicious prosecution provided 'some issue' encompassing these actions is revealed on the pleadings. But these are the only likely actions against the police which are specifically enshrined as of right by law. However, if other actions are included with the above, e.g. assault, then the whole case will be determined by a jury if one of the parties chooses to opt for one. An action for assault alone does not entitle a claimant to a jury trial and one is highly unlikely to be permitted, although there is a residual discretion to grant one (section 69(3)). The House of Lords have ruled in *Racz v. The Home Office* ([1994] 2 WLR 23) that the entitlement to a jury trial should not be extended to misfeasance where that is the sole cause of action but any case where *mala fides* against police officers is alleged strengthens the argument for the discretionary grant of a jury trial.

Should Claimants Opt for a Jury Trial?

The right of a jury trial has been retained in false imprisonment and malicious prosecution because of the important role members of the public should have in deciding factual issues between the police and their fellow citizens. Judges themselves are sometimes relieved to have this burden shifted from their shoulders. There was also a widespread perception that judges sitting alone would be biased towards the police. Whilst at one time there may have been more than a grain of truth in this, happily in the authors' more recent experience most judges have been meticulous in the search for the truth and have been far from shy in making findings against the police where warranted on the facts. However, we take the view that where there are substantial and serious allegations against police officers it is preferable for all concerned that the issues should be determined by a jury.

Where the situation involves rather more legal than factual issues, however, the case for a judge-only trial strengthens. This is particularly so in false imprisonment where the jury's role can be quite limited in cases where there is little factual dispute as to what information the police had to hand prior to making the arrest. It is then a matter of law for the judge to determine whether or not the arrest was unlawful. Indeed where there is no factual dispute then the jury has no role at all other than to determine damages. Thus careful consideration will have to be given as to whether it is appropriate to opt for a jury trial in those circumstances.

CHAPTER 5
COMMENCING A CASE UNDER THE NEW SYSTEM

OVERRIDING PRINCIPLES

The new rules, which came into effect on 26 April 1999, feature the following overriding principles.

1. **Co-operation**: to see if litigation can be avoided and, if not, working towards full and frank disclosure so that the parties can settle the case, if possible, at the first available opportunity.
2. **Proportionality**: the level of costs, work and disclosure should be proportionate to the relief sought in the case. For instance, the court is unlikely to want to spend three days arguing a case worth £50.
3. **Greater control**: this is to be exercised by the court itself. The court will no longer be prepared to rubber stamp orders but will instead expect the parties to explain themselves.

Solicitors will need to keep these principles in mind whenever any court procedure applies.

PRE-ACTION PRINCIPLES

Pre-action protocols will apply to all areas of practice and will govern the steps that should be followed prior to the commencement of any case. At present, there is no protocol for actions against the police, but attempts are underway to agree one. Even though there is no specific protocol, the rules provide that the nature and principles of other protocols should be applied. There is a protocol for personal injury cases and certain pertinent principles can be taken from that. In particular, the protocol suggests that two letters be sent before action to the other side is taken, setting out the substance of the case. Two letters are sent so that the police can forward one copy of the letter to its insurers or legal services department. The letter should be sufficiently detailed to make the case easily identifiable to the police and it may be advantageous to include some supporting documentation. This disclosure is required as it is designed to assist the police in assessing risk and, thereafter, liability.

After the letter has been sent, the client should wait for 21 days to allow the police to acknowledge receipt. If the police do not acknowledge receipt, the case can be commenced straight away. If, on the other hand, the police do acknowledge it, the client should give them three months to provide a substantive reply as to whether or not liability is at issue. If, after the three months have expired, the reply is not forthcoming, proceedings can be commenced. The reply should set out in sufficient detail why liability is in dispute. If the letter fails to do this, proceedings can be commenced.

Generally, it is agreed that the letter from the solicitor or his/her client will not be binding on the client and so the court documentation can change from what is contained in the initial letter. However, if the documentation is substantially different, the police could argue that they were not given proper notice of the case and adverse cost implications could apply.

The letter in reply, however, can be binding on the police if it contains an admission and if damages are valued at less than the £15,000. If the case is valued at more than this, the admission is not binding. Accordingly, the solicitor and client could attend court intending only to argue quantum. However, at court the police could say that they dispute liability and the solicitor could be expected to argue liability as well. If the solicitor is not prepared for this, the client could lose his/her case. Alternatively, the solicitor could prepare the case on liability as well as quantum only to find it was unnecessary. In the latter event, the police would obviously want to challenge any costs incurred in preparing the case on liability. This obviously is an unsatisfactory position and the solicitor should ask for clarification of the issue from the police.

Pre-action Disclosure from the Police

If liability is in issue, the client can now ask for relevant documents to be disclosed so that he/she can consider the police stance in detail and reassess the risk. It used to be the case that such documentation could not be obtained prior to the issue of proceedings in all but exceptional cases, but that has now changed. The position now is that the documents should be given and, if they are not, an application can be made to the court asking them to order it. In such cases, the court can order that the police pay the costs of the application.

If a party fails to comply with the nature of a protocol, there are no immediate sanctions that can be imposed; however, as the matter proceeds, the court will be entitled to take into account the parties' previous conduct in the case. Accordingly, the court will perhaps be less amenable in cases where there has been previous failure to co-operate. The failure or reluctance of the police to co-operate with pre-action disclosure would often present problems in the past. It is hoped that, in the future, solicitors will be able to get much more informaion about the potential strength or weakness of their case with these new procedures.

In certain cases, the client will not have enough time to allow three months for the consideration of matters as the time limit will be about to expire. In such cases, proceedings should be issued.

Alternative Dispute Resolution

This concept will be foreign to most solicitors who act for either party in these types of cases. It is, however, something that needs to be considered as it may provide a way forward. Schemes are being set up to allow potential mediation to occur. Their success will depend on the willingness of all parties to co-operate and a genuine desire to want to settle matters. This, unfortunately, has been a concept that has been absent for many years and is demonstrated by the fact that solicitors start a case a few yards away from each other, yet end it miles apart. This procedure is likely to be of limited use in cases against the police unless the client is only looking for an apology and a public statement putting the record straight; where it might be seriously considered.

ISSUING PROCEEDINGS

Three separate tracks will apply. You will need to decide which of these tracks is appropriate to your case. In reaching a decision, take note of the following principles:

1. Any cases under £5,000 in value will be allocated to the small claims track procedure.
2. Cases between £5,000 and £15,000 in value, which are relatively simple, and which can be heard in one day will come under the fast-track procedure.
3. Other cases, which are more complex and will require large amounts of oral evidence, will come under the multi-track procedure.

For police complaint cases, it is likely that unless they are very simple they will need to run in the new multi-track procedure.

Whether multi-track cases are commenced in the

County Court or the High Court will depend on the parties' own preferences, as the old differences are largely done away with. The principle of not commencing a personal injury case in the High Court, unless it is over £50,000 in value, continues to apply. Also, a case should not be commenced in the High Court if it is valued at less than £15,000.

Standard Claim Form

In order to commence any case (whether it is in the High Court, County Court or whether it is small, fast, or multi-track), you will need to complete a standard claim form. This form should include a full précis of the case and should, in particular, contain the following:

1. A concise statement of the nature of the claim.
2. The remedy sought.
3. A statement of value.
4. If a representative is commencing the claim, the capacity in which it is being commenced.

The statement of value should specify if the claim is for less than £5,000, between £5,000 and £15,000, or more than £15,000. In personal injury cases, you would state whether or not the claim is worth more than £1,000, as that remains the small track limit for those types of cases.

Valuing a claim can be difficult, especially in actions against the police, but the court will still require the solicitor to attempt it. The previous notes on valuing a claim should be referred to in this regard. See the Thompson Guidelines (in Chapter 2) for further assistance in this regard.

The solicitor should ask the client to sign the claim or obtain prior written approval from the client that it is correct. The actual statement itself should read as follows: "I believe that the facts stated in these particulars are true."

Particulars of Claim

In civil actions against the police, it is unlikely that the solicitor will be able to include the full nature of his client's case in the claim form itself. Accordingly, the solicitor will submit another document called a particulars of claim. This will set out in detail the full nature of the claim and the basis of the police misconduct. Any claim for aggravated or exemptory damages will also need to be particularised.

THE CONTENTS OF THE CLAIM FORM

The contents of the claim form and the particulars of claim will need to include a statement of what the case is and the interest and damages claimed (i.e. claim for assault and false imprisonment and malicious prosectutions). The idea is to fully particularise the claim in a simplified and easy to understand form. It is now possible to refer to your witnesses and to the items to be disclosed in support of your case in the documentation itself. You can also attach copies of the relevant documentation if you wish. This approach completely moves away from the legal jargon that formed the basis of pleadings in the past.

Timetable

The claim form needs to be served within four months of its issue. Where a statement of case is to be used, that statement will need to be served within fourteen days of the service of the claim form. In these types of cases, the solicitor will need to serve a copy of the statement of case together with a certificate of service at the court itself. These documents need to be lodged within seven days of serving the defendant with the statement.

Defence

The defendant will need to reply to the action in the same way as before by lodging a defence. That must be done within fourteen days of receiving the claim form. If a claim form and a particulars of claim are used, the defendant will need to lodge a notice of intent to defend within fourteen days, and the defence itself within 28 days. Time extensions can be agreed between the parties up to a maximum of 28 days. If more time than this is needed, the court's permission will be required. It will be clear from this that the defendant will be expected to move matters along expeditiously. The defendant will only have about four months from first finding out about the matter to filing a detailed defence. Accordingly, the police solicitors will need to move much faster than they have in the past.

The actual nature of the defence will be different. The defendant will now be expected to explain why he/she defends the case and the extent to which his/her version differs from the claimant's case. He/she will also have to mention the specific legal and factual defences to be relied upon. The defendant may also state that he/she disputes the statement of value as put in the statement of case.

As with the claimant, the defendant must specify if he/she is acting in a representative capacity and must verify that the contents of the defence are true to the best of his knowledge and belief. The following type of phrase may be used: "I believe (the defendant believes) that the facts stated in this defence are true." The solicitor should, however, get the client's written consent to this beforehand.

If the defendant fails to respond to the case, judgment may be obtained in default.

CHAPTER 6
INTERMEDIATE STEPS UNDER THE NEW SYSTEM

DISCLOSURE

The old discovery principle is replaced by the new concept of disclosure. Under the new rules, the level of disclosure that needs to be given is called standard disclosure. Under this, the following items will need to be disclosed.

1. All the documents on which the solicitor intends to rely.
2. All the documents that could adversely affect the client's case.
3. All documents that could assist the police case.

Standard Disclosure

The preparation of this disclosure schedule will occur as before by the preparation of a list of documents.

This new provision clearly imposes a duty on the police to consider all the unused material in cases to determine whether or not anything in the unused material could assist the client's case. This duty is limited by the new requirement that the parties conduct a reasonable search on behalf of their clients to locate the documents. Once this search has been completed, the parties will be required to provide a detailed statement setting out the extent of the search conducted. If the client feels that the search was not conducted properly or had shortcomings, he/she can apply to the court and ask for an interim order to be made that further enquiries are carried out. However, the guidelines for the search are restricted by what the court feels to be reasonable in the circumstances of the case. A court will not expect the police to carry out a search of documents involving hundreds of man-hours if the case is only worth a small amount of money. In such cases, the court would state that to expect the police to do this would be unreasonable, as the work involved was disproportionate to the remedy sought. In deciding what will be deemed 'reasonable', the court will be expected to have regard to the following factors:

- The number of documents involved;
- The nature and complexity of the proceedings;
- The ease or expense with which a document may be retrieved;
- The likely significance of a document.

If a party deliberately does not carry out a search of certain documents, it will be expected to specify what those documents are and why a search of them has not occurred. This will, ultimately, be open to challenge under the procedure described above.

It is likely that a lot of confusion will arise over this issue, and that what the client or his/her solicitor feels to be reasonable may not be the same as what the police deem to be reasonable. Disputes that arise out of this will be decided on a case by case basis until definite guidelines are laid down.

Specific Disclosure

In addition to the standard disclosure, there is also a new category called specific disclosure, which relates to other documents that the client may feel should be disclosed. In order to qualify for specific disclosure, an application, supported by a witness statement, will need to be made to the court. If it is granted, the party will be required to either disclose certain documents or make a search for them.

The right to apply for specific disclosure is very important as the right of the police to refuse disclosure on the basis of public interest immunity and/or privilege is preserved. Accordingly, the disclosure schedule prepared by the police is likely to continue to omit important information. In cases where public interest immunity is sought, the police will be expected to specify it and may be required by the court to lodge the document with the court so that a decision on it can be reached. (See 'Public Interest Immunity' below.)

The sanctions for not disclosing a document are that it be ruled inadmissible for the purposes of the trial. Solicitors should, therefore, take great care that all the documents upon which they want to rely at trial are disclosed. Also, they should ensure that they carry out a reasonable search for any other documents that may be relevant.

If a document that is subject to some form of privilege is inadvertently disclosed, it cannot be used at trial unless the court directs that it may be so used. This is important in larger cases where masses of paperwork exchange hands and inadvertently a document is disclosed which should not have been. Even though this principle provides protection, it does not prohibit use of the document altogether. Care should, therefore, be taken to ensure errors are not made as they could result in costly negligence cases arising.

Third Party Disclosure

Finally, in respect of disclosure, both parties now have the right to apply for disclosure from third parties unconnected to the case. In considering such matters, the court will have to consider whether disclosure is necessary to dispose fairly of the claim or to save costs. Again, it is unclear how this will be applied in practice. The ramifications for actions against the police may be quite substantial as they allow the client an alternative source from which to gather information. The relevance of any such application should be considered in each and every case, and are perhaps best borne out by way of an example.

> Assume that Mr A is alleged to have been seen by police officer B exposing himself in a park. Mr A denies this and alleges that the police are lying, as they do not like him. At trial, Mr A is acquitted and issues proceedings against the police. During disclosure, Mr A asserts that police officer B was on a training course with the territorial army on the day in question and seeks disclosure of the army's attendance logs for that day. Clearly, if the information is provided, it may save costs. It is also clear that the information may be necessary to fairly dispose of the matter. In such cases, the court may order third party disclosure, limited to whether police officer B was at the army training camp at the relevant time.

The party requiring third party disclosure will be the one expected to pay. The cost will depend on the level of disclosure sought.

PUBLIC INTEREST IMMUNITY

One problem which solicitors often come across in cases against the police is that the police will refuse to allow disclosure of some of the documents in their possession claiming they are covered by Public Interest Immunity (PII). The police are entitled to claim that it would be against the public interest for the claimant to see certain documents. If the claimant challenges this refusal to hand over the documents, the court will be required to balance the proper protection of confidentiality and state secrets on the one hand, and the prevention of the frustration of justice on the other.

The test is one of substance and not form. Thus, whether the document is marked 'state secret' or 'confidential' is not conclusive as to whether it should be disclosed. Nor does it matter that such disclosure might lead to criticism of a government department or the necessary attendance of government officials. Nor is PII even dependent on the objection of the police. It is up to the judge to decide if PII applies even where no objection is taken, although in practice this is unlikely to occur.

Principles of PII

The principles of PII were outlined by the House of Lords in *Conway v. Rimmer* [1968] 1 All E.R. 874 and *Burmah Oil Company Ltd v. Bank of England* [1979] 3 All E.R. 700. Historically, documents were divided into 'class claims' and 'contents claims'. If a particular document belonged to a 'class' of documents which would normally attract PII (e.g. documents subject to the Official Secrets Act, medical records, Social Services records), there is a presumption against disclosure, unless the claimant can persuade the judge that his/her case would be seriously compromised without it, and thus it would not be in the interests of justice. Even then, it may still be held to be in the public interest for such disclosure to be withheld. The burden of proof falls on the party refusing to disclose the document to show that it falls within this class in the first place. These presumptions are reversed in documents that do not come within the 'class' where PII would normally attach. In a 'contents' claim, it is presumed that disclosure will be made unless the objecting party can show that, in the particular case, it is in the public interest that it should be withheld from the other side.

While the distinction between 'class' and 'contents' claims still exists, the modern trend is to adopt a more flexible approach, judging each document on its individual merit.

Some Examples of Application of PII to Police Cases

Libel Documents

In *R v. Bromell* [1993] 1 All E.R. 86, it was held to be repugnant to justice to withhold documents which appeared to point to corruption on the part of named police officers in a libel action brought by those officers when they had already recovered substantial libel damages from other sections of the media.

Police Public Order Manual

In *Goodwin v. Chief Constable of Lancashire* (*The Times*, 3 November 1992), it was held that PII attaches to the Public Order Manual containing details of police public disturbance techniques on the basis that such information would provide valuable information to people intent on frustrating police control methods. However, disclosure could be ordered if it was otherwise impossible for the claimant to prove his/her case. This case illustrates the difficulty of trying to unearth any consistent principle of law on this topic.

Police Disciplinary Documents

The police often claim this immunity, and the courts have not always made consistent findings in this area. The position has now been restated by the House of Lords in *R v Chief Constable of the West Midlands ex parte Wiley* [1994] 1 All E.R. 703 and *R v Chief Constable of Nottingham ex parte Sunderland* [1994] 3 All E.R. 420. They held that there was no general PII in respect of documents coming into existence during an investigation against the police under Part IX of PACE. However, Lord Woolf recognised that there might be reasons, based on the contents of particular documents, why it would be appropriate to extend such immunity to a claim of PII on the 'contents' ground. Importantly, Lord Templeman said that "a rubber stamp approach to public interest immunity was neither necessary nor appropriate".

He went on to say that, while generally such police documents should be disclosed, they ordinarily should not "if they were sensitive police material relating to policy and operational matters". He drew a distinction between the evidence collected for the investigation that should generally be revealed, and the report of the inquiry which should generally not, unless it had particular relevance to the case in hand.

This distinction was emphasised in *Taylor v. Anderton and the Chief Constable of Manchester* [(Police Complaints Authority intervening) [1995] 2 All E.R. 420], where it was held that reports made by investigating officers on police conduct under Part IX of PACE formed a 'class' which was entitled to PII. Their disclosure would only be ordered where the public interest in their production out-weighed that of the preservation of confidentiality.

Sir Thomas Bingham M.R. justified the distinction between the report of the investigation and the evidence generated by the police inquiry, on the grounds that it was in the public interest "for investigating officers to feel free to report on professional colleagues without apprehension that their opinions become known to such persons". This immunity would also appear to cover reports sent from the police to the Crown Prosecution Service. This indicates that a report from a police disciplinary enquiry will be protected from disclosure but the evidence from it will not.

Police Informers

It has been held in numerous cases that there is a public interest in protecting the name of informers. For the police to be obliged to reveal the names of informers would not only put the informer at risk, but also dry up a very useful source of information to the police. Thus, the names will not be disclosed in civil proceedings unless there are extraordinary circumstances justifying it. This does not preclude the disclosure of the information itself, provided the identities can be concealed, if it is deemed relevant to the case.

Police Surveillance

For similar reasons, the names of persons who have lent their homes to the police to use for surveillance will not be revealed or any information which would lead to their identification.

Conclusion

The more flexible approach of the courts towards the question of disclosure, while being a very welcome development, nevertheless brings greater uncertainty as to what, in any particular case, the court will allow the claimant to see. Very few documents can now be shut out completely from consideration, particularly if they might have a decisive effect on the outcome of the case. Therefore, we advise that, unless there is an obvious and compelling reason why disclosure won't be made (e.g. a genuine case of national security or where the name of an informer would have to be revealed), the solicitor should always challenge the refusal of the other side to hand over a document and leave it to them to argue that it is covered by Public Interest Immunity.

WITNESS STATEMENTS

In the particulars of claim, the solicitor may specify who the witnesses are. It is, therefore, imperative that statements be taken at an early stage. The content of witness statements should take the following form:

- it should be written in the witness's own words;
- it should be short and simple yet covering the main issues in the evidence;
- it should contain a statement of truth.

If a witness statement cannot be taken, a witness summary may be obtained instead. In such instances, an application will need to be made to the court to use the summary instead of a statement. How this actually works in practice will need to be determined. The summary will need to specify the evidence, if known, which would otherwise be included and the name and address of the intended witness. If the evidence is unknown, the summary maker can specify the questions he/she would ask the witness if he/she had the chance. The police are likely to exploit this new mechanism to adduce evidence of officers who are either retired or have moved to other police forces. Where an application to use a summary has been made, the solicitor should clarify why a full statement cannot be taken.

Statements instead of Oral Evidence

In certain cases, the court may permit the witness statement to stand as direct evidence and so avoid the need for oral evidence to be heard. In these cases, a notice of intention to do this will need to be served on the other side, no later than the date for the filing of the questionnaire. On receipt of the notice, the other side will have fourteen days to apply to the court for an order to cross-examine on the evidence. If the court orders the witness to attend, the maker will be required to attend otherwise the evidence will be inadmissible.

Contempt of Court

It has been noted that a statement of truth will have to be included in the witness statement. If a false statement is made in the witness statement, the maker may be seen to be in contempt of court and, accordingly, be liable for prosecution. The solicitor should make clear to any witnesses and the client that this liability exists before obtaining their signatures. It should also be noted that counsel no longer sign the particulars of claim and thus the claimant can be directly cross-examined on the contents of the document which has been signed by him/her.

Finally, it will be noted that witnesses may choose to give evidence in the form of affidavits rather than a witness statement. Solicitors should note, however, that the fee for swearing the affidavit is no longer recoverable.

EXPERT EVIDENCE

There has been a significant change in the way that expert evidence is presented as evidence. One of the pre-action protocols is to look to instruct an expert who will act objectively on behalf of the court, rather than the individual parties; the court may direct how the costs of this should be split. If the parties cannot agree on an expert, the court may intervene and assist the parties in choosing an expert. In particular, the court can direct that an expert be chosen from various nominations supplied by the parties, or direct that the expert be selected in any way that the court chooses.

The parties will normally be expected to split the costs of the expert between themselves. Alternatively, the court can direct that the fees be split in some other ratio or order that a certain amount of money be lodged at the court.

Experts are only to be used if their instruction can reasonably be expected to resolve the proceedings. Care should be taken, therefore, to ensure that the use of an expert is necessary as the court may order that the expert cannot be used. In deciding this, the court will look at it on the basis of proportionality in respect of the whole case. Accordingly, the more complex a matter the more likely that expert evidence will be admissible.

As the expert is now acting for the court, he/she will be given the option of asking the court for further directions and, in certain cases, more time to prepare a report. The court will have to consider whether or not the application should be allowed as it may affect the key dates, as discussed in the Chapter 6.

Once a report is prepared, and regardless of whether or not it is from a joint expert or the other side's expert, the solicitor will be entitled to ask him/her questions. This is a completely new concept and provides an opportunity to obtain further and better particulars from the expert. The underlying principle behind this is that the parties will be able to clarify whatever they need, thereby avoiding the need to call the expert to give evidence in court. This opportunity can result in major breakthroughs and should be explored to the maximum.

The questions cannot, however, be used as a fishing expedition and must be directed at clarifying the report. The questions can be asked only once and will need to be put to the expert within 28 days from the service of the expert's report. The questions can, however, go further than what is necessary for clarification, if the court authorises that line of questioning or it is agreed between the parties.

Once the questions have been asked, the expert will be expected to reply to them. If the expert fails to do this, the court can order that the expert should not be paid and that the report be inadmissible. It is unclear who pays the extra costs for the work entailed in answering these questions, but it is likely that the party asking the questions will be expected to pay for them.

In replying to the questions, the expert will need to disclose the answers to both sides at the same time. Neither party should discuss the case with the expert as it may be suggested that an attempt has been made to affect the integrity and independence of that expert.

As has already been mentioned, in some cases the court may still allow the use of two experts, one for each side. In such cases, the court will expect the parties to identify what type of experts they require. Further, the court may expect the two sets of experts to get together to see if they can agree certain facts and, ultimately, either agree on a position or, alternatively, reduce the issues in dispute. In any event, the court's permission will be needed before any expert will be allowed to attend court to give evidence.

The content of the report should provide information on the following items.

- The expert's own qualifications.
- Details of the literature that he/she has relied on.
- Details of the tests that have been carried out together with details of the qualifications of the person carrying out those tests.
- A statement referring to the substance of the material relied on and details of whether it forms part of the report.
- A statement from the expert that he/she understands his/her duty to the court and that he/she has complied with that duty and disclosed all rel-

> evant material. This statement should also include a passage in which it is made clear that the conclusions reached in the report are valid in the light of all the material considered.

It should be noted that as disclosure of the instructions given to the expert can now be required, the solicitor will need to be careful about what he/she says in his/her instructions. The client should also be informed of this, as any rash comments made by him during the course of an examination could prove detrimental to the progress of the case.

Finally, in addition to the use of experts by the parties, the court now has the jurisdiction to appoint an expert of its own; if it considers it necessary for the fair disposal of a case. The expert is called an assessor and will be someone who has a certain skill or experience in a particular area. The court will determine the full extent of the role of the assessor, and he/she may be given leave to prepare a report and even attend trial. This approach may be extensively adopted by the court in actions against the police as they may want to have assessors appointed, such as blood splatter experts or DNA specialists. The costs incurred by the assessor are likely to be paid by the parties and the court will normally require the costs for the expert to be lodged at court prior to the trial.

From the above, it will be apparent that the whole system governing experts has been substantially changed. Solicitors should, therefore, take care when instructing an expert to ensure that he/she is fully aware of his/her obligations under the new procedures. Solicitors will also now need to consider whether an expert should be used at all and, if so, whether agreement can be reached with the police to split the costs.

CHAPTER 7
KEY DATES UNDER THE NEW SYSTEM

ALLOCATION QUESTIONNAIRE

Once the defence has been filed, the parties will be sent an allocation questionnaire (designed to allow the court to see which track is to be followed). This must be completed and sent back to the court.

The allocation questionnaire will have, in the top right-hand corner, a date by which it will need to be returned. This will usually be fourteen days after the service of the questionnaire. The claimant, when lodging the allocation questionnaire, will also need to lodge a fee of £80. Failure to lodge the fee can have dire consequences and result in the whole case being struck out. Obviously, this could amount to a very expensive mistake if the solicitor in turn is sued for negligence.

In deciding to which track to allocate the case, the following factors will be looked at by the district judge or master:

- the financial value of the claim;
- the nature of the remedy sought;
- the complexity of the facts and law;
- the views of the parties;
- the amount of evidence to be heard.

Often, in straightforward cases, the police may seek to have the case allocated to the fast-track procedure.

There are benefits in doing this, as the trial estimate will be reduced to one day. This will reduce the level of legal costs incurred. However, a client, or his/her solicitor, should consider whether he/she is happy to have the case heard in this way.

The most obvious benefit to the client is that the matter will be heard within 30 weeks and will be tied into a strict regime which determines what needs to be done and when. This may be highly attractive to some clients who are keen to get their matter heard as quickly as possible and who want to avoid protracted and complex litigation. Solicitors will need to discuss this matter with their clients and clients should be aware that they do not have to choose the multi-track procedure. However, the vast majority of cases against the police will be unsuitable for fast-track and as such multi-track should apply.

For the purposes of this book, the multi-track procedure is the one that is considered, as the fast-track is quite simple once you are tied into it. The issues of disclosure, witness evidence and other court rules, which have been discussed earlier, will equally apply to the fast-track as well as the multi-track procedures.

On the form, the parties are asked to specify the following.

1. Whether or not the pre-action protocols have been followed.

2. Whether or not either party is asking for summary judgement.

3. Details of the witnesses of fact.

4. Whether it is intended to instruct an expert and, if so, his/her name and field of speciality. The parties must also state if they intend to call the expert at the trial.

5. Where the trial is to be heard.

6. Details of the solicitor or barrister who will be presenting the matter to the court, and his/her dates of availability.
7. The likely length of the trial.
8. The likely costs of the whole matter proceeding to trial.
9. Any additional material that may be relevant.

From the above, it should be clear that both parties will be expected to know their case inside out by the time the pleadings have been exchanged.

The court will decide on the future conduct of the case, based on the information provided on the allocation questionnaire. Accordingly, the parties should have already considered all the papers by this stage and decided which witnesses will be relied on, even though discovery has not yet occurred. The emphasis will be on the parties to provide discovery at the protocol stage or, alternatively, to apply to the court for pre-action discovery. If this has not occurred, the client and his/her solicitor will need to specify in the allocation questionnaire that the witness lists may be altered at a later stage when full disclosure is given. The court, however, may be unhappy with this and may ask the parties to come before it and explain why they have not been co-operating. Cost implications may follow. In light of this, it is important that the parties are reasonable and work together to assist the court in delivering an efficient service.

Once the court has decided on the appropriate track to be followed, a notice will be sent out. The parties will also be sent a copy of the allocation questionnaire for their consideration. This is to ensure that there is transparency in the system and, hopefully, efficiency. On seeing the witness list, the parties will be able to determine the case against them. On seeing the predicted costs and doing a risk/return analysis, they can decide whether it is worth proceeding with the matter in light of the possible award of damages.

At the time of allocating the case, the court may decide that some other action should be taken, rather than simply allocating a track. In particular, the court may decide to criticise the statement of case or ask the parties for more details as to the nature of their case. Alternatively, the court may ask the parties to simplify their case and clearly set out which issues are in dispute. The court may also, of its own volition, order summary judgment or stay of action if it feels that the action should be put on hold for a number of months so the parties can try and resolve the matter amicably. On such occasions, the court can even give a preliminary view on the evidence at hand to encourage the parties to negotiate a settlement.

If a solicitor does not return the allocation questionnaire in time or fails to answer the questions properly, the court may ask him/her to attend court personally to explain what has happened. Again, cost penalties may be imposed.

Finally, if the defendant included a counterclaim, the allocation questionnaire and reply will need to be lodged at the same time. The claimant will also need to provide a certificate of service of reply to the court.

CASE MANAGEMENT CONFERENCE

If the case is to proceed under the multi-track procedure, a timetable will need to be set up which will govern the progress of the case; this will be done at the case management conference. This conference will be similar to a directions hearing but will have much wider scope. At the hearing, the court will look to set an agenda for the disclosure of documents, the exchange of witness statements, the exchange of expert reports and the reliance on them thereafter, the date for the pre-trial review, the date by which the listing questionnaire will need to be lodged, the date for the trial or a time bracket for when the trial will be heard. It will already be clear that a number of new things will need to be done, which have never been done before. Further, the days of the parties agreeing directions between themselves and asking the court to rubber stamp them are gone.

Some of the dates specified above will become key dates under the new procedure. The effect of this will be that the parties will be unable to change these dates without obtaining prior approval of the court, even where they agree it amongst themselves. Key dates include the dates for the pre-trial review, the lodgement of the listing questionnaire and the trial itself. The dates for disclosure, witness statement or expert reports exchange will be open to variation if the parties agree. The underlying principle is that the parties should be given certainty as to when their matter will be heard. Solicitors will not be allowed to be dilatory in their approach to cases.

The solicitor having conduct of the case should attend the case management conference as the court may ask trying questions about the case that a junior may not be able to answer. This could result in the matter being adjourned and costs awarded against the firm of solicitors.

It will be noted that the court may wish to discuss aspects of the case and may want to promote mediation or other forms of dispute resolution. Both parties should be prepared for this and be able to put forward arguments against it, if they feel it will be unsuitable.

LISTING QUESTIONNAIRE

This form will need to be completed by both parties once witness statements and expert reports have been exchanged. A court fee will be payable by the claimant at the time of lodging the form. This fee will vary between matters that are commenced in the County Court and the High Court, and should be checked directly with the court. Non-payment of the fee could be seen as a failure to comply with the need to lodge the listing questionnaire and could result in the case being thrown out. The date in the left-hand corner of the form will specify the deadline by which the form will need to be returned. That date will have been set at the case management conference.

The form asks the parties to specify:

a) whether or not the court directions have been complied with; and if not, why not?;

b) whether or not the court has given its consent to the use of expert reports and, if so, whether they have been agreed and whether leave is sought to call them to give evidence. If such leave is sought, the parties are expected to specify the dates of availability of those experts;

c) the names and addresses of any witnesses to be called, whether any of the witness evidence has been agreed and, for those whose evidence is in dispute, details of their dates of availability and whether they will require an interpreter;

d) details of who will be representing the client at trial together with his/her dates of availability;

e) details of any other relevant information.

From this list it will be clear that the solicitor will be expected to have spoken at length to the police in an attempt to agree much of the information requested above.

PRE-TRIAL REVIEW

Shortly after the listing questionnaire has been sent to the court, a pre-trial review will occur. This review will to go through the listing questionnaire to ensure that everything that needs to be done has been done and to ensure that there is no chance of avoiding a trial. The solicitor and counsel instructed should attend the review together with the client. The main reason for this is to give the court one last chance to settle the matter. At this juncture, the court may try to apply pressure on the parties by giving an indication of what they feel the likely outcome of the case will be, should it proceed to trial.

CHAPTER 8
PROCEEDING TO TRIAL

INTERIM REMEDIES

The court has wide powers to assist the parties in progressing a case, and has the jurisdiction to grant summary judgment. In addition to this, the court can order that the claimant's case is struck out. This new power in effect replaces the old power that previously existed under the principle of automatic strike out and under the principle of striking out for want of prosecution.

Under the new powers, a statement of case may be struck out if one of the following three criterion apply.

- Where the particulars of claim fails to disclose any reasonable ground on which to bring a case.
- Where there has been an abuse of the court process.
- Where there has been a failure to comply with a rule of court.

Solicitors should be wary of these rules as the court now has the power to make every order of the court an 'unless order', which means that failure to comply with it may potentially be seen to be an abuse of process. As this is criterion (2) above, it clearly could result in a case being struck out.

If a case is struck out, the costs of the action will need to be paid before any new action arising out of the same facts is commenced. If the costs have not been paid, the police could ask that the action be stayed until the previous costs are paid. Ultimately, this could result in the death of the action and give rise to a potential negligence action against the solicitor.

If the situation should ever arise that a solicitor is faced with the threat of having his/her case struck out, he/she should look at raising the following points in support of his/her case.

- Whether or not the failure was intentional.
- Whether or not there is a good explanation of what happened.
- Whether or not the trial date is going to be affected.
- Whether or not it is in the interests of the administration of justice.
- Whether or not there is a record of previous lapses.

Regarding the last of these points, the court will look at whether the pre-action protocols were followed as well as other court orders.

In addition to striking out a case or giving summary judgment, the court also has wide powers to govern disclosure. This is not just limited to pre-action discovery but applies also to specific disclosure as discussed in Chapter 6. Under the new rules, the court has power to order disclosure where one party has access to documents or information that the other side is unlikely to have. In such cases, the court can order the party with the information to prepare and file a statement recording the information and serve a copy of that document on the other side. Further, the court has wide power to order a party to clarify any matter in dispute or give additional information relating to any matter which is contained or referred to in the pleadings. If such disclosure is ordered, it will need to be served together with a statement of truth. This, in effect, is a statement confirming that the content of the statement is true. This power, in effect, replaces the old system of requesting further or better particulars or asking for interrogatories. The new system suggests that a written request for the information should be made and should, thereafter, be followed by a request to the court, if the police refuse.

In order to apply for an interim remedy, you would normally lodge an application at the court supported by evidence which stipulates the information you require and the reasons for it. The evidence is to be in the form of a witness statement rather than an affidavit. The reason for this change is that it is felt that unnecessary fees were being incurred in having affidavits sworn. The maker of the statement, who will either be the client himself or the solicitor, will also need to provide a statement of truth.

Once the application has been lodged, a date will be set down for hearing the matter and the parties will be asked to attend the court. If there is an objection, a reason will need to be provided which will have to be considered by the court. After that a decision will be made in the usual way.

Finally, an interim application can be made to the court without notifying the other side. This should, however, only be done when there is a clear urgency and that the delay caused in making the application on notice to the other side would cause prejudice to that party. In such applications the court will need to be told of the reason for the urgency.

OFFERS TO SETTLE/PART 36 OFFER

Under the new procedure, either party can now make an offer to settle the whole or part of the proceedings. The defendant will usually do this by making a payment into court, and will also be able to do this by way of a letter. This is very similar to the previous situation, with the difference now being that the client can suggest to the police that he/she would be prepared to settle proceedings if a certain amount of money is paid. The police will need to take care in refusing this offer as, if it is beaten at the eventual trial, they may be ordered by the court to pay interest on those damages from the date of the offer, at a rate which is 10 per cent above the base rate. Additionally, the costs of the solicitor will be calculated by the court on the indemnity basis rather than the standard basis. What this actually means in practice is that, if there is a dispute over a certain cost, it will be decided upon in the favour of the party receiving the money, rather than the party claiming it. Effectively, this means that the solicitor is likely to get a large part of his/her costs, if not all of them, from the other side.

The police will not want to be stung in this way and, as such, will need to give serious consideration to the offer.

The offer itself (whether it is made by the police or the client/solicitor) can relate to an issue in dispute, part or all of the claim. It will need to specify what it relates to and the amount being offered. It will also need to be left open for 21 days.

The court, in deciding whether to order interest in the punitive way, will take into account the terms of the offer and the conduct of the parties and all other relevant material.

Solicitors should use this approach to apply pressure on the police to settle matters and should appraise their clients and the legal aid board of the effects of any such offer that is made to them.

SETTING THE MATTER DOWN

Once the pre-trial review is over, the matter will proceed to trial. The use of a witness summons/subpoena will still apply. The hearsay notices will also remain.

The court bundle will need to be filed at the court not more than seven days but not less than three days before the start of the trial. The contents of the bundle will need to include a copy of the following.

- A case summary of not more than 250 words.
- The claim form and particulars of case.
- Any requests for further information of the particulars of case.
- The defence.
- Any requests for further information of the defence.
- All the witness statements.
- Witness summaries, if any.
- Any notices to adduce hearsay evidence.
- Plans and/or photographs.
- Medical reports and responses to them.
- Other expert reports and responses to them.
- Orders of the court.
- Other documentation to be relied on.
- Any notices such as notice of issue of legal aid.

The expert reports can be included in a separate bundle if they are voluminous. They should be cross-referenced with the other bundle and different coloured folders should be used. If the bundle of documents is over 100 pages long, dividers should be used to split up the different sections. The content of the bundle should be agreed wherever possible. The original documents should be taken to court so that the court can look at them if it chooses.

TRIAL

The procedure surrounding the trial itself has not changed. Fast-track cases will be expected to last no more than a day; however, the conduct remains as it was before.

COSTS

As of 1 March 1999, new rules came into force to deal with the issue of costs. In particular, the costs of any interlocutory hearing will be settled at the end of the hearing and will become payable within fourteen days. Non-payment of costs could result in the action being put on hold and, ultimately, thrown out. *It should be noted that this rule does not apply to legally aided clients.*

In order to allow the court to consider the issue of costs, a new duty is imposed on the parties to prepare a schedule of all costs incurred. The breakdown of the costs will need to be supplied to the other side 24 hours before the hearing together with details of the hourly rate applied and any enhancement sought. If this information is not supplied, the court may reduce the level of costs that are recoverable. The principle behind this is that the parties will be more likely to settle matters if they can physically see money coming out of their pockets.

Even though the costs issue is currently limited to interlocutory hearings, the intention is to expand it to all hearings, including trials. This will result in costs being determined there and then. This may ultimately benefit solicitors, as it will do away with the need to wait for taxation of costs to occur.

A specimen format for detailing costs is set out on page 93.

COSTS OF HEARING

Attendances	**Fee Earner Status**	**Time**	**Cost**
Client			
Opponent			
Counsel			
Witness			
Preparation			
Counsel's Fee			
Other Costs			
TOTAL			

FAST-TRACK

The directions that will apply after the allocation has been made are as follows.

1. Disclosure should occur within 4 weeks.
2. Witness statements should be exchanged in 10 weeks.
3. Expert reports should be exchanged in 14 weeks.
4. Listing questionnaires should be filed in 22 weeks.
5. The trial should be heard in 30 weeks after the date of the notice of allocation.

Fixed costs will apply to the trial. If the damages are between £1,000 and £5,000 (in personal injury cases), the fixed fee will be £350. Damages between £5,000 and £10,000 will result in fixed costs of £500. For damages over £10,000 fixed costs of £750 will be recovered. If the solicitor chooses to use counsel to represent the client at the final hearing, the solicitor may be allowed to recover a fixed cost of £250, for his/her own attendance, if the court approves. Any ongoing action which was issued before the 26 April 1999 is governed under the transition criteria.

TRANSITION CRITERIA

A. Any action that continues beyond 25 April 1999 cannot be automatically struck out.

B. Any undefended cases will continue under the old rules until they are concluded.

C. All defended cases will be governed by the new rules. If a writ or County Court summons has been issued but there is no defence, the new rules will apply automatically and the defence should be filed at the court so that the allocation questionnaire can be sent out.

D. If the pleadings have been concluded, the old system of directions should not be applied; instead, an allocation questionnaire should be completed and lodged at the court.

E. If the directions stage has already been reached, the directions should continue unless there is a need to vary them. If the matter does come before the court under these provisions, the court will bring the case under the new criteria. Any application made to the court will be made under the new procedure. If the matter is proceeding before the High Court, copies of all pleadings will need to be lodged at the Court so that the file will be available for consideration. Once the directions have been completed, a listing questionnaire should be lodged so that the matter can come before the Court.

F. In any event, if a district judge comes across a file during the course of court business he/she can, of his/her own volition, transfer the matter to the new list and send out notice to the parties.

G. If any procedural step has been passed, the parties will not be expected to revisit it. Accordingly, if the parties have already exchanged witness statements and reports, they will not be expected to exchange them again, under the criteria of the new rules.

H. If the matter is ready for trial it will proceed, but its conduct will need to be in accordance with the new rules.

I. If judgment has been obtained in default under the old rules, the police will need to apply to have it set aside under the new rules.

APPENDICES

APPENDIX 1
POLICE POWERS IN RELATION TO SEARCH WARRANTS

As we have seen, the police now use their many powers of arrest without a warrant to effect most of their arrests. However, warrants still play an important role in relation to the searching of property. Here we summarise the main application and execution provisions together with the appropriate Code of Practice Guidelines issued under PACE. In practice, the police must follow these guidelines as well as the procedural steps in the Act in order to render the warrant and search lawful. Any wrongfully issued warrant and/or unlawful searching constitutes a trespass to either property or person.

The warrant conditions should be strictly construed and any warrant is automatically invalid if it is executed on the wrong person or at the wrong address.

The police must restrict their search to what is listed on the warrant and not indulge in a 'fishing expedition', still less a ransack.

PACE has given the police new powers of search under sections 17, 18 and 32. Section 17(5) abolishes the old common law powers of constables generally, but their power of entry and search to prevent a breach of the peace is retained.

The police have been granted many other statutory powers of entry and search in specific Acts, perhaps most notably under the Misuse of Drugs Act 1971.

Section 15 (Application for a Warrant)

This section states:

> An entry on a search of premises under a warrant is unlawful unless it complies with this and section 16.

The section lays down the following procedural requirements.

- It is the constable's duty to state the grounds on which he makes the application, the enactment under which the warrant would be issued, the premises to be searched and, as far as possible, the articles or persons to be sought.
- The application to the magistrate must be made *ex parte* and in writing.
- The constable must answer on oath any questions put to him by the magistrate.
- The warrant can authorise only one entry.
- Two copies must be made of the warrant and the copies must be verified as such.

Code of Practice B

Police officers are obliged to comply with these guidelines when applying for a warrant under section 15.

- The officer must take reasonable steps to check that the information is accurate, recent and has not been provided maliciously or irresponsibly. An application may not be made on the basis of information from an anonymous source where corroboration has not been sought.
- The officer shall obtain as specifically as possible the nature of the articles and their location.

- The officer should make reasonable enquiries to establish what, if anything, is known about the likely occupier of the premises.
- An application must be made with the authority of at least an inspector or the senior officer on duty.
- If there is reason to believe that a search might have an adverse effect on relations between the police and the community, the liaison officer shall be consulted before the search takes place or, in urgent cases, as soon as practicable after it has happened.

Section 16 (Execution of a Warrant)

This section stipulates:

- the warrant must be executed by a constable, unless other persons are specifically authorised by the warrant;
- execution must be within one month from the date of issue;
- entry and search must be at a reasonable hour;
- if the occupier is present, the constable shall:
  a) identify himself to the occupier and provide documentary evidence that he is a constable if he is not in uniform;
  b) produce a warrant to him;
  c) provide him with a copy of the warrant.

Code of Practice B

In addition to section 16, PACE has a Code of Practice that the police are obliged to follow when executing a warrant. This code stipulates:

- where the premises are occupied, the constable shall identify himself by the warrant number and show the warrant card if he/she is not in uniform and explain the purpose of the search and the grounds for undertaking it;
- the officer in charge shall first attempt to communicate with the occupier or another person entitled to grant access by explaining the authority under which he seeks entry unless:
  a) the premises to be searched are known to be unoccupied;
  b) the occupier and any other person entitled to grant access are known to be absent;
  c) there are reasonable grounds for believing that to alert the occupier or any other person entitled to grant access by attempting to communicate with him would frustrate the object of the search or endanger the officers concerned or other persons.

Note:
This last provision is often used by the police to justify ignoring most of the other safeguards, particularly in drug raids where they invariably force their way in unannounced using battering rams. This provision does not give the police *carte blanche* to smash their way into people's homes regardless of the individual circumstances. When the police use this part of the Code to justify actions of this type, they must be able to satisfy a court, if challenged, that such tactics were reasonable in the circumstances and the normal procedures laid down by section 16 and the Code of Practice were not viable options.

APPENDIX 2
DETENTION WITHOUT ARREST: STOP AND SEARCH

PACE has granted the police greatly increased power to detain people against their will, in public or in a vehicle, for the purpose of searching. The police can exercise this power not only without a warrant but also without an arrest. This gives the police a wide area of discretion as to how they choose to exercise this power and, in most cases, the citizen has little chance to challenge either its use or abuse.

A detailed Code of Practice has been drawn up under PACE which is designed to discourage police officers from 'stereotyping' certain groups, e.g. racial minorities and youths who wear unconventional hairstyles or clothing. However, the extent to which the police have resisted the temptation to 'pick on' certain groups is a matter of no small controversy. Annual figures and various surveys have indicated that not only do the overwhelming majority of these 'stops' fail to produce anything of any evidential value, but also that people from racial minorities figure disproportionately among the general public inconvenienced in this way.

We include here both the statutory power and the relevant Code of Practice. Any breach would constitute a technical assault but, more importantly, might be a consideration in deciding whether the police have behaved lawfully in respect of a particular person. An action for misfeasance might lie against officers who repeatedly 'targeted' a person in breach of the Act and the Code.

THE SEARCHING POWERS

Section 1(1) of PACE gives the police power to stop and search without having to make an arrest in any place where the public have access. The constable may search:

- any person or vehicle;
- anything which is in or on the vehicle;
- for stolen or prohibited articles or articles listed in section 1(8).

Section 1(7) 'Prohibited Articles'

The articles mentioned in this section include:

- an offensive weapon;
- an article made or used in the course or in connection with an offence to which 1(8) applies.

Section 1(8)

The offences for which the above apply are:

- burglary;
- theft;
- taking motor vehicles without authority;
- obtaining property by deception.

Section 1(8A)

This was added by section 140 of the Criminal Justice Act 1988 and gives the constable power to search for any bladed article which is an offence created by section 139 of that Act.

Lawfulness of Search

Section 1(3) states that in order to be acting lawfully the constable is required to have reasonable grounds for suspecting that such articles will be found.

DOCUMENTATION

Sections 2 and 3 lay down detailed requirements that the constable has to undertake both before and during the search and the subsequent documentation which are largely reflected in the Code of Practice below.

Road Checks

Section 4 gives the police power in certain circumstances to conduct road checks to ascertain if a vehicle is carrying a person who:

- has committed an offence other than a road traffic offence;
- is a witness to such an offence;
- is intending to commit such an offence;
- is unlawfully at large.

Section 4(4) limits these powers by stating that they may only be exercised after written authorisation by an officer of the rank of at least superintendent (unless in an emergency (4(5)) and only after he/she has reasonable grounds for believing:

- the offence is a serious arrestable offence
- that the person in question is in the locality.

Code of Practice A

This Code states that:

- the police must have reasonable grounds for suspicion that articles unlawfully possessed are being carried;
- the suspicion must have some objective basis for it;
- reasonable suspicion can never be supported by personal factors alone, e.g. colour, age, hairstyle, manner of dress, or that the person is known to have previous convictions. Nor must there be stereotyped images of certain persons or groups more likely to commit offences;
- where an officer has the reasonable grounds for suspicion necessary to exercise a power of search, he may detain the person concerned for the purpose of, and with a view to, searching him. There is no power to detain a person against his will in order to find a ground for searching him in the first place;
- before carrying out the search, the officer may ask any question of the person. If reasonable suspicion no longer exists as a result of that questioning, any detention for the purpose of a search is unlawful and cannot be retrospectively provided by such latter questioning.

The officer has to supply the following information to the person being searched.

- Basic information including:

  a) the name and name of police station;

  b) the object of the search;

  c) the grounds for undertaking it.

- The officer must make a record of the search and inform the person concerned that he is entitled to a copy of it if requested within a year, unless it is not practicable to make a record (what constitutes 'impracticability' is not elaborated upon).

- Every reasonable effort must be made to reduce the embarrassment that a person being searched may experience.
- Co-operation should be sought. A forcible search may only be undertaken if the person clearly demonstrates that he is not going to be searched voluntarily. Reasonable force only may be used.
- The time taken for a search must be reasonable and not extend beyond the time necessary for the search. The thoroughness and extent of the search depends on the circumstances.
- The search must be conducted at the place where the person was first detained or nearby.
- Searches in public must be reduced to superficial examination of outer clothing. There is no power to require the removal in public of any clothing except an outer coat, jacket or gloves. Where, on reasonable grounds, it is considered necessary to conduct a more thorough search, this should be done out of public view. Any search involving the removal of more than an outer coat, jacket, headgear or footwear may only be made by an officer of the same sex as the person being searched and only done in the presence of a person of the same sex unless the person searched makes such a request. (It should be noted that the distinction between "superficial examination of outer clothing" and "a more thorough search" is not made clear).
- A written record of the search must be made as soon as practicable on a form provided for the purpose.

SPECIFIC STATUTORY POWERS OF STOP AND SEARCH

In addition to the powers granted under PACE, the police have been given specific stop and search powers without arrest by other statutes. Below is a summary of the main ones.

Act	Object of Search
Section 47, Firearms Act 1968	Firearms
Section 23, Misuse of Drugs Act 1971	Controlled Drugs
Sporting Events Act 1988	Intoxicating Liquor (on persons, coaches and trains)
Section 164, Customs and Excise Management Act 1979	Imported prohibited drugs.

APPENDIX 3
TIME SPENT IN CUSTODY

PACE has laid down strict time limits as to how long a suspect should spend in custody without being charged. There are also mandatory reviews that the review officer is required to conduct. PACE also sets out strict conditions that must be satisfied before an extension can be granted by a magistrate in the case of a serious arrestable offence.

While PACE does not give a person the right per se to take an action for breach of this part of the Code or the Act, any detention beyond what is permitted will, it is submitted, clearly be an unlawful imprisonment.

Primary Rule (sections 41 -45)

No suspect is to be kept in custody without charge for more than 24 hours.

Extension for Serious Arrestable Offences

A superintendent or more senior officer may authorise a further twelve hours if he/she has reasonable grounds for believing that the following conditions are met.

1. The detention of that person is necessary to secure or preserve evidence relating to an offence for which he/she is under arrest, or to obtain such evidence by questioning him/her; *and*

2. The detention of that person is necessary to secure or preserve evidence relating to an offence for which he/she is under arrest or to obtain such evidence by questioning him/her; *and*

3. The relevant offence is a serious arrestable offence; *and*

4. The investigation is being conducted diligently and expeditiously.

Thus all four conditions must apply before the extension is lawfully granted.

Detention without Charge beyond 36 Hours

Detention beyond 36 hours may be authorised by a warrant of further detention granted by a magistrate who can authorise a further extension. A magistrate can authorise an extension of up to 90 hours on further application. The suspect must be present during the hearing and have the opportunity to make representations either personally or through legal representatives.

No extension of time beyond 90 hours without charge is permitted.

GENERAL MATTERS

- Time starts when the suspect arrives at the police station or the time of arrest, whichever is the earlier.
- The time includes being taken to hospital by the police for treatment after arrest.
- At the expiry of the 24 hours (or later if extended), the detained person must be either charged or released.
- A person so released shall not be re-arrested without a warrant for the offence for which he/she was being detained unless new evidence justifying a further arrest comes to light since his/her release.

REVIEWS

A review officer must undertake reviews in custody. For a person who has not been charged, the review officer must be someone of the rank of at least superintendent who is not involved in the investigation. For someone who has been charged, the review officer is the custody officer.

First review	6 hours after arrival at the police station
Subsequent reviews	9 hour intervals

Postponement is permitted if:

- the suspect is being questioned and the review officer is satisfied that the interruption would prejudice the investigation;
- no review officer is available – this must be recorded on the custody record.

The Substance of the Review

The review officer must give either the detained person (unless sleeping), or his/her legal representative an opportunity to make representations about the detention. These can be made orally or in writing. The review officer must satisfy himself/herself that continued detention is necessary. If the suspect has been detained 'for questioning', and he/she either has already been fully interviewed or he/she is not to be interviewed at all, his/her continued detention will be unlawful in the absence of a charge, release on bail or unconditional release.

APPENDIX 4
THE POWER TO TAKE FINGERPRINTS AND PHOTOGRAPHS

FINGERPRINTS

Sections 61(3)(a) and 67(4) of PACE permit the police to take fingerprints without consent, if an officer above the rank of superintendent has reasonable grounds for believing that the suspect is involved in a criminal offence, and that the fingerprints will either prove or disprove his/her alleged involvement.

Thus, there is no general power for the police to take fingerprints of arrested persons. Any such taking without consent in circumstances that cannot be lawfully justified would constitute an assault.

Code of Practice D

This Code states that:

- a suspect must be informed that his/her fingerprints will be checked against others;
- an officer must take all reasonable steps to try and persuade the suspect to co-operate with the taking of a fingerprint, if he/she is refusing to do so;
- force must be both a last resort and reasonably applied in the circumstances;
- all fingerprints and all copies must be destroyed as soon as practicable if the suspect is:

a) prosecuted and cleared of the offence;

b) not prosecuted.

However, no such destruction is required where someone admits an offence and is cautioned.

There are special provisions relating to terrorist offences.

Recordable Offences

In the case of a person who has been convicted of a recordable offence (as defined in section 118) and who has not had his/her fingerprints taken, section 27 of PACE empowers the police to require him/her to attend a police station at a specified time and place for the purpose of having his/her fingerprints taken, provided:

- less than a month has elapsed since the conviction;
- the suspect has been given seven days' notice;
- a constable may arrest without warrant anyone who refuses to comply.

PHOTOGRAPHS

The police have no general right to take photographs of arrested people without consent. They are specifically prohibited from taking them by force by the relevant *Code of Practice D* which states that:

- a photograph may only be taken with the suspect's written consent unless D.4.2. applies;
- the suspect must be told the reason why a photograph is required and that he/she may witness its destruction or be provided with a certificate con-

firming its destruction within five days of being cleared or informed that he/she will not be prosecuted.

D.4.2.

This stipulates that a photograph can be taken without written consent if:

- the suspect is arrested at the same time as other people or at a time when it was likely that other people would be arrested and a photograph is necessary to establish who was arrested and at what time and at what place; *or*
- the suspect has been charged with, or reported for, a recordable offence and has not yet been released or brought before a court;
- the suspect is convicted of such an offence and his/her photograph is not already on record. (There is no power of arrest under this provision and it only applies if the person is in custody as a result of another power.);
- an officer of at least the rank of superintendent authorises it, having reasonable grounds for suspecting the involvement of the person in a criminal offence and where there is identification evidence in relation to that offence;
- force may not be used to take a photograph. (The Code does not say how the police can take a photograph 'without consent' but 'with no force' in circumstances where the suspect completely refuses to co-operate, e.g. by pulling his/her shirt over his/her face – presumably it permits the taking of a covert photograph.)

When a person's photograph has been taken under D.4.2., all photographs, copies and negatives taken in that particular case must be destroyed if the suspect:

- is prosecuted and cleared unless he/she has a previous conviction for a recordable offence;
- has been charged but not yet prosecuted for an offence.

APPENDIX 5 CHECKLIST: WORKING YOUR WAY THROUGH A CASE

INITIAL WORK

1. Has the franchise form been completed?

2. Give the dates upon which the franchise form has been checked and updated.

Date	**Fee earner update**

FUNDING LITIGATION

3. Is the client private paying?

   Has he been advised of the anticipated final cost?

   Has money been obtained on account? If so, how much?

Dates on which interim bills sent	**Amount**

4. Are we instructed on a no win fee arrangement?

   Has a risk analysis been carried out and a success fee agreed?

   Has the client signed a conditional fee agreement in accourdance with the Law Society guidelines?

   Has insurance been obtained for the client?

   Have monies been placed on account for disbursements? If so, how much?

5. Does the client enjoy the benefit of legal aid?

   What are the limitations on it?

Cost	**Authorised to do**

Have checks been made to determine whether the client's financial means have changed?

Date of check	**Fee earner**	**Result**

PRELIMINARY ENQUIRIES

6. Have the tapes of the interview been obtained? If so, have they been listened to?

7. Has the custody record been obtained?

8. Have the section 9 witness statements been obtained and considered?

9. Have the exhibits been obtained and considered?

10. Has the unused material been considered?

11. Has a CAD printout been obtained?

12. Have copies of the client's medical notes been considered?

13. Has the client provided his/her comments on the prosecution papers?

14. Has a background statement been taken from the client?

15. Have full details of the client's loss been clarified and receipts/proof been obtained?

16. Have the client's witnesses been identified? If so list name and details of whether a statement has been obtained.

Name of witness	**Date statement taken**

17. Has a plan been prepared?

18. Have photographs been taken?

19. Have instructions been sent to counsel to advise on the merits of the case?

20. Has counsel advised about proceeding with the case?

FIRST CONTACT WITH THE OTHER SIDE

21. Has a letter before action been sent in accordance with the protocols?

    Date of sending letter

22. Has the defendant replied to the letter within the requisite 21 days? If so, what is the date before which no further action can be taken?

    Date for next action

23. Has a substantive reply been received which deals with the basis of the action? What is the defence?

24. Is there any disclosure that needs to be obtained from the police? Identify the documentation so required.

25. Have the police agreed to give voluntary pre-action disclosure? Has an application for pre-action disclosure been considered and made?

26. Has the new material obtained been considered?

27. Has a decision been made to issue proceedings?

28. Has all the evidence been reconsidered and the main issue in the case identified? Specify the issue.

29. Which witnesses are to be relied on for the purposes of the trial? Specify them.

Witness name	Statement of truth obtained (Y/N)

30. Has a claim form been completed together with the particulars of case? Has it had the statement of truth signed by the claimant?

PLEADINGS

31. What date was the claim form lodged?

32. What date was the particulars of case lodged?

33. What date is the defence due?

34. What date was the defence received?

35. What date is the allocation questionnaire due?

36. What date was the allocation questionnaire returned to the court? Was the fee paid?

37. Is there going to be an allocation hearing? If so, when?

38. What is the allocation for the case?

39. If the case is to be fast tracked please specify the following:

Date due	Date done
Disclosure	
Inspection	
Exchange of witness statement	
Exchange of expert report	
Questions for expert	
Listing questionnaire	
Agreeing bundles	
Lodging bundles	
Trial	

40. If the case is multi-track, specify the date for the case management conference.

41. What directions are we asking for from the case management conference? Specify the following:

    Summary judgment

    Clarification of defence

Disclosure: level standard
specific

specify date

Inspection

Exchange of witness statements

Expert: which ones?

are they to act for both sides?

who is to pay?

Jury/Judge only trial

Cagegory of trial judge

Representation

Listing questionnaire

Pre-trial review

Trial

42. What directions were ordered by the court?

DISCLOSURE

43. What date is disclosure due?

44. Have we advised the client of the duty imposed upon him/her to make a search?

45. Has the client made a search and signed the disclosure document regarding the existence of other documents?

46. Are there any class of documents which we should not disclose, as disclosure of them would be unreasonable? If so, specify.

47. Are we satisfied with the level of disclosure received by us?

48. Do we need to make an application for specific disclosure? If so, what are we asking for?

WITNESS STATEMENTS

49. Who are our witnesses? Specify.

50. Have we advised each of the witnesses about the statement of truth?

51. Have the witnesses all signed their statements and the statement of truth?

52. Are their any witness summaries to be relied on? If so, specify.

53. Is there any hearsay evidence? If so, has a hearsay notice been prepared?

54. What is the date for the service of witness statements?

55. Have we received the witness statements from the defendant?

56. Have the witness statements been checked and solicitors' comments prepared on them?

57. Have the witness statements been checked against the documents provided on disclosure to check if there are anomalies?

58. Have the client's instruction been taken on the disclosure documents?

59. Have the client's comments been taken on the witness statements? (All of them?)

EXPERT REPORTS

60. Have we instructed an expert?

61. Do the police have a separate expert?

62. Have both parties instructed a joint expert?

63. Has the expert's initial report been received and checked?

64. Have we asked the expert all the questions on which we require clarification?

65. Has the final report been received (whether joint/separate reports)?

66. Has the client's instructions been taken regarding the expert report?

LISTING QUESTIONNAIRE

67. What date is the listing questionnaire due?

68. Has the listing questionnaire been lodged and has the fee been paid?

PART 36 OFFER

69. Has counsel been briefed?

70. Has a conference been arranged with counsel?

71. Has advice been obtained regarding potential settlement figures?

72. Have instructions been taken from the client regarding the proposed settlement figure?

73. Has a part 36 offer been made?

74. What has been the outcome of the part 36 offer?

75. Do we need to take further instructions from counsel and the client regarding potential settlement?

PRE-TRIAL REVIEW

76. What is the date of the pre-trial review?

77. Is counsel available to attend the review?

78. Are there any outstanding matters which need to be resolved? If so, specify?
79. What was the outcome of the pre-trial review?

PREPARING FOR TRIAL

80. What date is the trial?
81. Have we reconsidered all of the evidence? Is there any other work that should be done?
82. Have we prepared all the notices to admit documents?
83. Have we prepared a case summary?
84. Have we prepared a chronology?
85. Have we prepared a schedule of case law?
86. Have we agreed the trial bundle?
87. Have we lodged the trial bundle at court?
88. Have we served a copy of the trial bundle on counsel and the other side?
89. Have we warned our witnesses for the trial?
90. Have we gone over the witness statements with our witnesses prior to the trial?

91. Have we gone through all the evidence with our client on last time?

92. Have we held a conference with counsel and the client?

93. Are there any last steps which need to be taken as a result of this conference?

94. Would counsel benefit from a *locus in quo* visit?

95. Have we prepared a breakdown of our costs to date?

96. Have we served the other side with an estimate of costs prior to the hearing?

97. Have we received a breakdown of the defendant's costs?

98. Have we prepared a list on behalf of the defendant to challenge their costs if necessary?

99. Do we have details of any part 36 offers that have been rejected?

INDEX

THE STRESS BARRIER:
Nature's Way to Overcoming Stress

Pradeep Chadha

Organisations with a highly stressed workforce show decreased levels of risk taking, more missed opportunities, distortion of communications and more industrial relations problems. Employee performance and productivity suffers, absenteeism tends to increase, morale declines and creativity decreases.

The Stress Barrier looks at meditation, relaxation, psychology and medication, explores how these areas inter-link with successful stress management, and also exploring the mechanisms linking philosophy and spirituality. It looks at the various functional areas of stress, such as depression, post-traumatic stress, anxiety and addiction, and helps readers identify these problems and start to overcome them.

The book includes a series of simple exercises which will help readers identify, and start to sort out, their particular stress related problems. It will prove to be vital reading for anyone who feels that they may be suffering from stress due to the ever-increasing demands put upon them in today's competitive working environment, and also to managers and company directors who need to know what to do to sort out the problem of a workforce which may be in danger of succumbing to stress-related under-performance.

The Author:
PRADEEP CHADHA is a Stress Management Consultant, based in Dublin.

160 pages
1-901657-65-5; £14.99; pbk; September 1999

THE BLACKHALL GUIDE TO EMPLOYMENT LAW IN THE UK

Lynda Macdonald

Employment, and the law relating to employment, is vitally important. Responsibility for this increasingly important area is often devolved to line managers nowadays.

The Blackhall Guide to Employment Law in the UK is a generalist employment law book, aimed at managers and supervisors, covering their legal and managerial responsibilities towards their staff, and covering all aspects of employment law. The book is written from a practical standpoint, rather than from a legal theory standpoint. It includes numerous case studies, which explain, clarify and expand on the points raised and show how best practice works in action.

The book covers:

- Contracts of employment
- Continuity of service
- Breach of contract
- Terms and conditions of employment
- Hours, holidays and time off
- Pay and benefits
- Sex and race discrimination
- Maternity rights
- Disability discrimination
- Sickness benefits
- Sensitive issues
- Termination and redundancy

The Author:
LYNDA MACDONALD is a human resources consultant, based in Aberdeen.

248 pages

1-901657-62-0; £19.95; paperback; May 1999

LAW AND THE FAMILY IN THE UK

Maureen Mullally

Every day of the week, in family courts in every town and county, men, women and children come face to face with the law. *Law and The Family in the UK* deals with the law as it relates to families, and in particular as it relates to divorce and separation. The book includes up-to-date information on Legal Aid, the Child Support Law, and The Children Act. It deals with the many practical issues that need to be faced up to by people who are looking into the idea of getting a divorce or a legal separation.

The book answers all the important questions raised including:

- How to go about getting a divorce
- What rights people have if they are living with someone and decide to separate
- What preparations are required before an appearance in court
- The expense involved in the legal process
- How the law can help people to escape from a violent relationship
- What steps people can take if they think their child is being abused

Law and the Family in the UK cuts through the legal jargon and explains in clear, user-friendly and understandable language what to do when family relationships break down, and how to understand the law in this area.

The Author:
MAUREEN MULLALLY is a practising barrister who has specialised in family law for over twenty years. She is a member of the Family Law Bar Association.

210 pages
1-901657-53-1; £9.99; paperback; April 1999

The above books can be purchased at any good bookshop or direct from:

BLACKHALL PUBLISHING
26 Eustace Street
Dublin 2
Ireland

Telephone: +353 (0)1-677-3242; Fax: +353 (0)1-677-3243;
e-mail: blackhall@tinet.ie